Psychotherapy
and
Spirituality

Perspectives on Psychotherapy

editor: Colin Feltham
Sheffield Hallam University

Each book in this challenging and incisive series takes a particular perspective on psychotherapy to place it in its intellectual and cultural context. Disciplines which will be brought to bear in this series will include sociology, anthropology, philosophy, psychology, science and feminism.

Books in the series

Philosophy and Psychotherapy
Edward Erwin

Psychotherapy and Society
David Pilgrim

Feminism and Psychotherapy
edited by
I. Bruna Seu and M. Colleen Heenan

Therapy Across Culture
Inga-Britt Krause

Psychotherapy and Science
Robert Langs

Psychotherapy and Spirituality
William West

Psychotherapy and Politics
Nick Totton

Psychotherapy and Spirituality

Crossing the Line between Therapy and Religion

WILLIAM WEST

SAGE Publications
London • Thousand Oaks • New Delhi

First published 2000. Reprinted 2001, 2002

 SAGE Publications Ltd
6 Bonhill Street
London EC2A 4PU

SAGE Publications Inc
2455 Teller Road
Thousand Oaks, California 91320

SAGE Publications India Pvt Ltd
32, M-Block Market
Greater Kailash – I
New Delhi 110 048

British Library Cataloguing in Publication data

A catalogue record for this book is available
from the British Library

ISBN 0 7619 5873 8
ISBN 0 7619 5874 6 (pbk)

Library of Congress catalog card number 99–073866

Typeset by Mayhew Typesetting, Rhayader, Powys
Printed in Great Britain by Biddles Ltd, *www.biddles.co.uk*

I dedicate this book to the memory of my mother Margaret Ethel West (1911–92) who taught me more about spirituality than I usually know.

Contents

Acknowledgements

Any book like this one that takes a long time to incubate leaves the author struggling with whom to acknowledge. Firstly, this book would never have appeared without the active encouragement and support of my editor Colin Feltham and of Susan Worsey at Sage. My colleagues Dr Henry Hollanders and Mary Berry at the Counselling Research and Training Group at Manchester University were invaluable and very understanding, especially during a period of study leave. The therapists who participated in my researches into therapy, healing and spirituality have made a huge contribution, especially the members of the PsychoSpiritual Initiative, but must inevitably remain anonymous.

A number of the ideas in this book were thrashed out in doctoral supervision sessions with Professor John McLeod, in seminars with various groups of students, and in presentations at various conferences including SPR (International) at Salt Lake City (1998), the Durham International Counselling Conference (1998) and the BAC Research Conference (1997).

I have been much influenced by contact with a number of people including: Linda Ankrah, Allen Bergin, Joy Dickinson, David Hay, Enid Hughes, Grace Jantzen, Kate Keogh, Bruce Liese, Fiona Moore, Clark Moustakas, David Orlinsky, Abdullah Popoola, Colin Purcell-Lee, David P. Smith, Richard Summers, Mary Swale (who gave valuable comments and feedback on a late draft of the book), Brian Thorne, Brian Wade and Alex Wildwood, none of whom should be held responsible in any way for the contents.

Figure 6.1 'A multilevel multidimensional assessment strategy', copyright American Psychological Association 1997, and Table 7.1 'Prayer behaviours in order of frequency', copyright Jessica Rose 1993, are reprinted with permission.

Finally my thanks to my wife without whom little of this would be possible. During the course of writing this book my daughter Emily Grace was born. She has had a huge impact on my life including my limited grasp of spirituality.

Introduction

The Zeitgeist is now ripe for the integration of a spiritual strategy into mainstream psychotherapy theory and practice. (Richards and Bergin, 1997: 48)

It is essential to place counselling in a religious perspective because the concepts of conscience, covenant, community, altruism, love, confession, enlightenment, and many others are so central to religions and have obviously informed counselling theory and practice. (Feltham, 1995: 93)

Counselling and psychotherapy have a problem with spirituality: it does not easily fit in with the professional and secular image that many therapists seek to present to the world. Many follow Freud in being dismissive of religion and of spiritual experiences. Few counsellor and psychotherapist training programmes include any mention of spirituality as a healthy part of human life despite the research evidence to the contrary, and despite the expressed wishes of many trainee therapists that their courses include a consideration of spirituality (Swinton, 1996).

Often when I lecture to a group of trainee or qualified counsellors I ask them to do an exercise in which I invite them to rate on a scale of 1 to 5 how important religion is to them, with 1 being not important, 5 being very important. Invariably the mean turns out to be just over 3, that is religion has some importance to these counsellors and trainee counsellors. I then invite them to do the same task but substituting the word 'spirituality' for 'religion'. The mean is usually over 4, that is spirituality is of importance to the group and usually at least one point higher on average than religion.

As it turns out both clients and therapists continue, like the rest of the population, to have spiritual experiences, though many clients remain too inhibited to raise such matters with their therapists. The process of therapy itself can, at times, have an overtly spiritual dimension to it: indeed, it is possible to view therapy as a spiritual process.

MY POSITION

In my professional therapeutic life I have worked under various labels including therapist, psychotherapist and counsellor. Although there are some differences between the practices of counsellors and psychotherapists, I find within Britain there is a great deal of overlap. Indeed, I regard the qualifying labels such as 'cognitive-behavioural', 'psychodynamic' and 'humanistic' as clearer separators than the words 'psychotherapist' or 'counsellor'. In this book I will tend to use 'therapist' to cover both counsellor and psychotherapist.

In my therapy, teaching and research work I seek to be open to what people are telling me. That is I try to 'bracket', to set aside my own biases, preoccupations and cultural framework, and to understand what is said to me within the other person's frame. Total bracketing, as John Heron (1992) reminds us, is impossible: indeed to attempt it itself represents something of a new frame. In approaching the whole question of spirituality it seems exceedingly difficult not to take a stance at all.

I am also aware that in the memorable words of Denzin (1989) 'gender filters knowledge' and that whatever I write here reflects that deep truth. Similar statements can be made in relation to race, class and culture.

It may prove helpful if I name some of my biases and frameworks. I am male, white, middle class, heterosexual, a father and a therapist turned academic, and I was born into an implicitly Christian household. I went to a Church of England primary school, and a Methodist Sunday school for a while. I was baptized into the Church of England at puberty after a serious illness and confirmed soon afterwards. (Confirmation is the formal process of becoming a member of the Church of England. It involves a period of instruction followed by a special public ceremony in which the person being confirmed is blessed by a bishop.) I gave up regular churchgoing when I reached university.

In my 20s and 30s I read a fair number of heretical Christian writings and the work of other writers on Christianity (including Jung, 1968; Pagels, 1982; Reich, 1952). I was also influenced by meeting some members of the Matriarchal Study Group in 1979 and by reading some of the history of the worship of the Goddess in ancient and more modern times (Graves, 1961; Stone, 1976). In my 30s, working as a humanistic body based therapist (West, 1994), I became interested in the flow of energy in the body and outside and this later led me to become a spiritual healer. During my 30s I pursued a vaguely New Age form of spirituality based on experiencing spiritual energies until by accident I found myself at a Quaker meeting at the outbreak of the Gulf War. The same spiritual energies were present there and I felt I had found my spiritual home. Along the way I have soaked up some of Buddhism including meditation practices.

I was recently in York for a meeting with colleagues and having a few minutes to spare I decided to visit the Minster or cathedral. As I entered the church I immediately felt a sense of being in a spiritual place: if you like, I was awestruck. I made for the small chapel that I knew was set aside for silent prayer. Inside the chapel I was overwhelmed by the feel of the spiritual energy present and was moved to weep. I felt such a sense of gratitude at being able to feel this energy and also had a sense of being enabled to return to my true nature or spiritual self. This was immediately followed by a feeling of regret at not living enough from that true centre of mine. I spent some time in prayer for those close to me, especially those in difficulties, and also spent time in contemplation. I left the Minster feeling uplifted and cleansed and somewhat washed out.

This was yet another spiritual experience for me of a kind that occurs relatively frequently during Quaker services, and when visiting churches and other holy sites which can include stone circles like Stonehenge and Avebury. Such experiences can occur during quiet moments alone in prayer, meditation or contemplation. Sometimes I have a strong sense during such experiences that changes are occurring in my energy field or aura. With my eyes closed or sometimes open I 'see' amethyst coloured light that swirls around the front of my face. This might seem a strange phenomenon but others have reported the same (see Summers, 1997). The sense of a return to my own true nature during such spiritual experiences is a regular feature of such events for me.

As a therapist I work within a humanistic way, drawing on what I know to help my clients explore what is important for them. A humanistic approach is essentially an integrative or eclectic way of working in which the therapist draws on a variety of humanistic techniques in order to benefit the client (West, 1999b). This often involves the spiritual even if it is not always named as such. Since 1995 I have taught on a counsellor training course that, whilst deeply humanistic in orientation, uses Egan's (1990) three-stage skilled helper model, which incorporates techniques drawn from a cognitive-behavioural approach where useful. It is from this integrative working perspective that I offer this book.

THE PARADOX OF SPIRITUALITY AND PSYCHOTHERAPY

One of the important contributions that the mathematician and philosopher Bertrand Russell made to mathematics was what is called Russell's paradox, which in mathematical terms goes: does the set that consists of those sets that are not part of themselves include itself? Most of us find this hard to make sense of. At a social gathering, when asked to explain it, Russell gave the following colloquial version. Imagine a small village in which the local barber shaves every man except those men who shave themselves. Does the barber shave himself? 'Of course he does,' is the immediate answer, but then you realize he only shaves those who do not shave themselves. So of course he does not shave himself, and then you realize he does shave those who do not shave themselves: hence the paradox.

This conveys for me something of how difficult it is to approach this issue of spirituality, especially in relation to psychotherapy. If I start out as a man of spiritual faith and knowledge, taking the view that spirituality is something in which we all live and move and have our being, then psychotherapy becomes subsumed in spirituality. However, if the function of psychotherapy involves questioning and interpreting our deepest beliefs in the light of modern secular psychology, then spirituality becomes subsumed within psychotherapy. Either can put the other under the microscope, but when does the process end? How do we bottom out on it? Which ultimately is the container of the other? I experience a great reluctance to have to choose which is the container of the other and perhaps the best solution is for it to be context based, that is: in what setting am I operating – as a therapist or as a spiritual director? However, even that solution is not in reality so simple, as will become clearer in subsequent chapters.

There is a paradox about spirituality and how I think I and many others talk about it. Firstly, everything can be seen to be spiritual, that is we are spiritual beings on a spiritual journey inhabiting a spiritual universe. Secondly, although I do regard myself as being on a spiritual path, I lose sense of this truth: I regard some special experiences and key moments as spiritual, and the rest of the time I can feel somehow less than the true spiritual being I know myself to be. I have elsewhere explored this gap in relation to my spirituality as lived out in my workplace (West, 1998d). So in this book I am often using spirituality in this second sense, sometimes in the first sense, and sometimes both!

What This Book is and is Not

This book explores how therapists might include the spiritual dimension within the therapeutic relationship and the implications of that inclusion. It proposes that therapy can be seen as a spiritual process and draws out the implications this has for therapist, client and the wider world. It is not written from the viewpoint of a religious conviction although my own religious beliefs mentioned above will impact on the text. It is also not written from within the transpersonal or Jungian frameworks although it is influenced by them. It is not primarily written from an analytic viewpoint although my own therapeutic practice has been informed by an' ever deepening understanding of some key analytic concepts such as transference, countertransference and projection. It is written from a broadly humanistic position in which the basic questions are posed: what is your story, how do you experience it, what difficulties in your life have brought you to therapy? This is definitely not a book on pastoral care or spiritual direction although again it may show my exploration of that territory, and will probably have much to say of value to those involved in pastoral care. There is a huge overlap between spiritual direction and therapy, and this book is written from the therapy viewpoint in a way that includes the spiritual.

What is in This Book?

Chapter 1 provides an overview of many of the main themes of this book including the nature of spirituality and the relevance of religious and mystical experiences. The legacy of Freud's negative view of religion is addressed, as is the question of why therapists need training in dealing with spiritual issues. The current state of the Christian Churches in Britain is explored briefly before recognition is made of the importance of traditional forms of healing or shamanism. Chapter 2 focuses on therapy and spirituality, opening with a brief historical summary of the development of psychotherapy and counselling from the perspective of their religious roots. It then considers the main schools of therapy and their relationship with spirituality including multicultural and religious therapies, before exploring what we know about the faith of therapists. Chapter 3 deals with some current issues in therapy, dwelling on the limits of secular therapy, our empty or saturated selves, before exploring the opportunities presented by spirituality, including whether we can regard therapy itself as a spiritual practice.

Chapter 4 considers religion in Britain today, recognizing the decline in conventional religion, the rise of fundamentalism, new religious movements, New Age spiritual practices, and do-it-yourself spirituality, before finally acknowledging the role of 12-step and other self-help programmes with a spiritual emphasis. Chapter 5, which appeared in an earlier form as a paper to the Durham Conference (West, 1999a), explores spiritual experiences in therapy, considers the implications of the therapy space being seen as a spiritual space and addresses the concept of spiritual unfolding.

Chapter 6 invites therapists to meet the challenge of spirituality and issues around spiritual awakening and emergence including those of assessment, spiritual addiction and countertransference. This is followed by a consideration of therapists' own spiritual development, highlighted by a case study of one psychotherapist's spiritual development. Next, how to map the psychospiritual is explored. The chapter ends with a brief overview of the value of a phenomenological and existential approach to therapeutic work.

Chapter 7 continues the theme of meeting the challenge with a consideration of spiritual interventions that therapists could make, contra-indications for such interventions and the supervision issues that can arise around spirituality in therapy. I then present five case examples drawn from my own practice that highlight and illustrate the use of spiritual interventions and spiritual understanding within therapy.

Chapter 8 then explores and answers some of the main criticisms of considering spirituality in therapy. Chapter 9, the concluding chapter, addresses themes around the future of therapy as a spiritual activity including the meeting place and difference between spiritual direction and therapy, and how therapists can address the totality of people's lives. At this point very necessarily the supervision dilemmas and issues around therapy and spirituality are considered, together with a focus on the ethical and boundary issues involved. Finally, an agenda for change is proposed and the wider implications are considered.

GENDER, RACE AND CULTURAL ISSUES

As already stated I agree with Denzin (1989) that gender filters knowledge. How we approach spirituality, our discourse about it, our way of viewing the divine, all reflect this. Taking the last point, does one actually acknowledge that there is a divine being? The Buddhists don't as such. Is the divine being to be found only inside us, or only outside us, or both? What name do we give to the divine being? And what does that name · imply? For example in the recent Swarthmore Lecture (Young Friends General Meeting, 1998) we find: 'Some of us have taken to using the spelling "Godde" instead of "God", pronounced the same, to dissociate the experience of the numinous from the hierarchical and patriarchical image of a "jealous, vengeful man in the clouds".'

The Church of England is still coming to terms with its recent ordination of women. It still does not dare appoint women as bishops and struggles with any real acceptance of homosexuality and lesbianism, especially among clergy. It is perhaps not surprising that it is in many ways mirroring similar conflicts within the larger secular culture, except that the Church of England like the monarchy often seems to lag behind popular opinion.

Those of us who claim to have spiritual experiences will often maintain that the experience is beyond words (Hay, 1982; Wilber, 1983), and beyond mind. However, it is inevitable that once we begin to talk about such experiences our language is culturally based. Spirituality does not stand alone or above everything: once it is talked about it is in a cultural context.

The spiritual journey, like its secular counterpart the voyage of self-discovery, involves probably the whole range of human emotions from joy and bliss through to rage and anguish. This book, with its emphasis on psychotherapy, perhaps focuses too much on the difficulties associated with the spiritual path rather than on the bliss of the mystical state or the joy of worship of the creator. As already mentioned, such states are notorious for being difficult if not impossible to put into words.

To those who might question the whole purpose of this book I can best borrow David Lyall's words: 'there can be few counsellors in any context who do not bring to their task both a world view and a personal agenda that transcend the simple application of technique' (1995: 55). I would suggest that to ignore or denigrate one's clients' spirituality is to do them a deep disservice. Indeed such behaviour may be viewed as being unethical. This book addresses many of the key questions involved in therapists being open to their clients' spirituality and spiritual journeying.

1

An Overview

It is not true that we have to give up the concern for the soul if we do not accept the tenets of religion. (Fromm, 1950: 9)

In the pastoral and spiritual context an understanding of what it means to be human cannot be contained solely within psychological models. (Lyall, 1995: 80)

It is now common for people to present themselves to therapists with concerns that they themselves have categorised as specifically spiritual in nature. (Thorne, 1998: x)

Psychotherapy, many would argue, is scientifically informed . . . With this frame of reference, religion or spirituality is the enemy. (Heelas and Kohn, 1996: 294)

This chapter sets the scene by considering what spirituality is before exploring religious, spiritual and mystical experiences and their relevance to modern psychotherapy. No discussion of spirituality and psychotherapy can avoid recognizing Freud's negative view of religion which reflected the ascendancy of science over religion at that time. We next address the question: why do therapists need training in working with spiritual issues? This tension between therapy and religion is then sited within the historical context of the split between science and religion and the decline of Christianity and conventional religion in the UK. Finally we explore the phenomenon of shamanism as an example of how spiritual techniques from aboriginal cultures are being applied in Western societies.

WHAT IS SPIRITUALITY?

'Spirituality' seems to be one of those words, like 'love', that have great importance to many people but whose meaning is hard to pin down. Many people when talking of spirituality will say that it is beyond words: indeed it is as if people run out of words, or find themselves in a territory where words fail them, or even do not exist. Another key point that arises time and again when talking about spirituality is that it is not the same as religion.

As a starting point it will be of use for us to explore what is meant by the word 'spiritual'. My position is not one of 'proving' that spirituality exists, or convincing the reader that this is the case. My concern is this: many people regard their spirituality as of crucial importance to them, and therapists need to recognize this fact and the implications it has for their work. Therapists may feel that the spiritual experiences of which their clients speak can be understood in non-spiritual language but this would be to deny them their words. Religion and spirituality offer a number of sets of words and frames within which to make sense of our spiritual lives. Of course we do not have to explore this and many therapists choose this option. However, if therapists do not, then it is important they recognize this limit to their competence and interest.

The word 'spiritual' is given a range of meanings within therapy and therapy related literature, varying from all forms of self-awareness (Farrow, 1984) to all states of awareness which possess values higher than average (Assagioli, 1986). Personal development as a whole is regarded by some as intrinsically spiritual, while others would limit the word 'spiritual' to those developments that take us beyond secular Western therapy. A number of writers and researchers have explored what is meant by spirituality and spiritual or mystical experiences (Allman et al., 1992; Assagioli, 1986; Farrow, 1984; Hardy, 1979; Maslow, 1970; Thomas and Cooper, 1980; Wilber, 1983).

In the mid 1980s at Pepperdine University a team of researchers under the guidance of Professor Elkins (Elkins et al., 1988) decided to explore spirituality from a humanistic and phenomenological perspective, which neatly fits in with the approach of this book. They investigated what people mean by the word 'spiritual' and produced the following definition:

> Spirituality, which comes from the Latin *spiritus*, meaning 'breath of life', is a way of being and experiencing that comes through awareness of a transcendent dimension and that is characterized by certain identifiable values in regard to self, others, nature, life, and whatever one considers to be the Ultimate. (1988: 10)

It is interesting to compare this definition with that provided by Alister Hardy, the founder and first director of the Religious Experience Research Unit at Oxford in 1969. One of the key features of Hardy's work there was to gather first-hand accounts of religious experience from thousands of people. He concludes:

> It seems to me that the main characteristics of man's religious and spiritual experiences are shown in his feelings for a transcendental reality which frequently manifest themselves in early childhood; a feeling that 'Something Other' than the self can actually be sensed; a desire to personalize this presence into a deity and to have a private I–Thou relationship with it, communicating through prayer. (Hardy, 1979: 130)

Both definitions mention the transcendent dimension and both allude to something ultimate, though in Hardy's definition it is taken further into a mention of a deity (where that leaves Buddhists is another matter). Hardy also specifies prayer as a channel of communication with the deity.

RELIGIOUS, SPIRITUAL AND MYSTICAL EXPERIENCES

> Putting words to religious experience is notoriously difficult. (Hay, 1982: 157)

> Religious, and especially mystical experience has had a profound impact on psychotherapy, and in many ways the therapists' agenda to induce radical transformation of the personality can be equated with just such religious states. (Feltham, 1995: 99)

It is very difficult to define what religious, mystical and spiritual experiences are and then to separate them out from each other. Indeed David Hay and Anne Morisy in their seminal work 'Reports of ecstatic, paranormal, or religious experiences in Great Britain and the United States – a comparison of trends' (1978) highlight this dilemma in the very title of their paper.

We find, for instance, that spiritual experiences often seem to result in a change of values (Elkins et al., 1988) as do 'mystical' experiences (Allman et al., 1992; Pahnke and Richards, 1966), which are often defined in similar if not identical terms. If we compare, for example, Elkins et al.'s (1988) and Thomas and Cooper's (1980) definitions of spirituality and spiritual experiences with Allman et al.'s (1992) definition of mystical experience, we find several common factors. These include transcendence, change in values, and feelings of sacredness.

Thomas and Cooper (1980) explore the difficulties in defining intense spiritual experiences, which they say might be referred to as 'cosmic consciousness', 'transcendent', 'mystical', 'peak', 'religious' or 'spiritual' experiences. They usefully distinguish between spiritual experiences categorized as mystical, psychic, faith, consolation and uncodable.

For many, the concept of the spiritual is closely associated with notions of higher ethical values, even though the record of many who claim spiritual development does not always illustrate such values in action, for instance the Crusades, or the persecution of witches (Spanos, 1978). This association is encompassed by Elkins et al.'s (1988) definition of the word 'spiritual', included in the previous section, which is difficult to better.

To help clarify this whole area of religious and spiritual experiences I will focus mainly on the work of Professor Elkins and his team who sought to define spirituality, and the work of David Hay into religious experience, before briefly considering mysticism. Professor Elkins and his team were seeking a definition of spirituality from within a humanistic-existential approach: 'In our work we have striven for an enlarged definition of spirituality that would not equate it with narrow religious beliefs, rituals, and practices' (1988: 7–8).Their work was based on four major assumptions: that there exists a spiritual dimension; that spirituality is a human phenomenon and potentially exists in all people; that spirituality is not the same as religiosity; and that spirituality can be defined, described and assessed.

To further develop their understanding of spirituality Elkins et al. (1988) made a study of the literature. From the literature they distilled nine major components which they tested out on five people noted for their spirituality who described themselves as Buddhist, Catholic, Protestant or Jewish. Indeed Elkins et al. (1988) present the notion that spirituality is a multidimensional construct consisting of nine major components. These are in summary:

1 *a transcendental dimension* exists and can be experienced whether as personal God, a transcendent dimension, Greater Self etc.
2 *meaning and purpose in life*, that the 'existential vacuum' can be filled with an authentic life
3 *mission in life*, that the spiritual person has a vocation
4 *sacredness of life*, that life is infused with sacredness and the spiritual person can experience awe, reverence and wonder even in non-religious settings, and that all of life is holy
5 *challenging material values*, that ultimate satisfaction is to be found not in materials but in things of the spirit
6 *altruism*, being affected by the pain and suffering of others, having a sense of social justice and that we are all part of creation
7 *idealism*, having a vision of a better world and a desire to bring it about
8 *awareness of the tragic*, that pain, suffering and death are part of life and give it colour and shade
9 *fruits of spirituality*, that being truly spiritual changes all aspects of who we are and how we live.

This is a fairly comprehensive list of some of the likely topics that can arise around spirituality within the therapeutic or spiritual direction relationship.

Returning to Elkins et al.'s (1988) brief definition of spirituality, some comments are in order. Firstly, *awareness of a transcendent dimension* draws our attention to the fact that people experience spirituality as an altered state or transcendent dimension. Secondly, the mention of *a way of being and experiencing* is crucial. We find that public opinion surveys in the USA and in the UK (Hay, 1982; Hay and Morisy, 1978) show that up to one-third of the adult population have had religious or spiritual experiences at some point in their lives, even in the UK where traditional church attendance is at a low ebb. So such experiences do not correlate with church attendance and appear to be cross-cultural (Hay, 1982), and can happen to agnostics or even atheists. Thirdly, the mention of the Ultimate invites us to consider God(s) and Goddess(es) and the possibility that the divine could be found within.

Elkins et al. end the report of their study with the following words which speak eloquently of the challenge facing us if we are truly to be open to each other's spiritual lives:

In our day the traditional religion has failed to meet the spiritual needs of many people. In their quest for a life of depth and meaning, it seems there is a growing number who are pursuing alternative spiritual paths and nurturing their spirituality in ways they are discovering for themselves. The spiritual development of these people deserves to be treated with respect and sensitivity by those studying spirituality. (1988: 16–17)

Turning to a consideration of the work of David Hay, it is worth reflecting that humankind has always expressed an awareness of there being a sacred presence in the world as far back as written records go and possibly earlier: 'Religion is a well-nigh universal phenomenon, occurring in some form in practically every culture' (Hay, 1982: 23). This does not necessarily make it true or valuable. It is also not to say that every person would feel thus: indeed by the late Victorian era it was clear that the Christian Church in Britain was in decline (and it continues to decline) and that religious beliefs were increasingly open to question.

However, it is important that we distinguish between religion as an institution and people's own sense of religiosity or spirituality. According to David Hay (1982) people are reluctant to disclose an ecstatic, paranormal or religious experience. Consequently it has only relatively recently become apparent how common such experiences are. David Hay's own opinion poll survey (Hay and Morisy, 1978) found that one-third of the people who were asked, 'Have you ever been aware of being influenced by a presence or power, whether referred to as God or not, which was different from your everyday self?', answered yes. However, when individual qualitative interviews were used an even higher number replied in the affirmative (Hay, 1979; 1982), again reflecting the taboo around such disclosures.

It is worth noting that one-third of the therapists taking part in my research into therapy and healing, although not a random group by any means (West, 1995a), reported feeling the presence of God sometimes in their work, and over three-quarters had, on occasion, felt part of something bigger than themselves and their clients.

Hay's survey found that 'people reporting religious experience are significantly more likely to report a high level of psychological wellbeing than those who do not' (Hay and Morisy, 1978: 259). Such experiences were also found to correlate positively with age, education, class and living rurally or in a small town. A similar figure of one-third reporting such experiences was obtained in the USA in a survey undertaken by Greeley (1975). However, Americans are three times more likely to be members of a Church or church service attenders than people in Britain. Although there was some correlation between church attendance and having religious experiences, Hay found: '45% of churchgoers do not claim experience and a large number of non-churchgoers, including atheists and agnostics, do claim it' (Hay and Morisy, 1978: 264).

It appears that people have such experiences irrespective of their beliefs. It is then a matter of what they make of such experiences, and what they do about them. Some people will fit them in with their religious beliefs, some will not, some will not even regard them as religious or spiritual. Most will keep such experiences to themselves. Indeed David Hay (1982) comments that this taboo on talking about religious experience is reminiscent of that which used to surround sexuality, and perhaps reflects the long history of tension between mystics and the Christian Churches.

Indeed many fear being taken to be mad. Clergy are not always sympathetic or understanding of such phenomena, and we find that: 'On the whole, 20th Century secular society appears intent on avoiding this area: consequently it offers no genuinely integrative interpretation, but reduces it to something meaningless or symptomatic of illness' (Hay and Morisy, 1978: 266). Indeed for Freud the true substance of religious experience was a psychotic hallucination (Hay, 1982).

Hay (1982) is convinced that the universality of religious experience and its continuing survival as a phenomenon irrespective of church attendance points to its value to us as a species. It contradicts the expectation that religious feelings were something we would evolve out of. Consequently Hay poses the question: what is the value of such experiences? His answer, backed up by others including Elkins et al. (1988), is that religious experiences often result in an ethical shift in the person concerned. This shift is away from materialism and towards altruism. Hay reminds us of how much we need such a shift given the global problems we now face. Such a viewpoint is increasingly common among ecologists (see Lovelock, 1979) and among people professing New Age Spirituality (Ferguson, 1993).

What are the implications of this? As we have seen, David Hay insists that spiritual experiences are cross-cultural and do not correlate with church attendance and that at least one-third of the population at some point in their lives will have such experiences. What implications might this have for practising therapists? One answer is provided by Allman et al. (1992) who did a survey of 650 members of the American Psychological Association who were in full-time practice. From the 285 respondents it emerged that 4.5 per cent of their clients (931 out of 20,670) had reported a mystical experience to them in the previous year; 67 per cent of the respondents had had such a report from one or more clients. The definition of mystical experience used was:

> a transient, extraordinary psychological event marked by feelings of being in unity and harmonious relationship to the divine and everything in existence, plus one or more of the following effects: noesis, religiosity, loss of ego, time and space alterations, ineffability, affect change during the event, transformation effect and passivity, i.e. experiencing no control of the event. (1992: 565)

No similar survey of the attitude of therapists to mystical experiences has been done to my knowledge in Britain. However, drawing on Hay's work we would expect a somewhat similar figure of about 4–5 per cent of clients in any one year, with the phenomena being reported to about two-thirds of therapists within any one year. Although such experiences are often not troubling to the person involved they sometimes can be. In either case the mystic experiences often have great impact, suggesting that the person involved is likely to welcome the opportunity to explore the experience. Clearly it is a matter to be considered in therapist training programmes.

No psychological exploration of religious experience and mysticism would be complete without reference to the pioneering work of William James whose seminal work was *The Varieties of Religious Experience* (1901). James pointed out how 'mysticism' and 'mystical' are often used as terms of mere reproach. He puts forward four defining features of a mystical experience which remain relevant. These are:

1 *ineffability*, that mystical states cannot be explained only experienced
2 *noetic*, that mystical experiences appear to be states of knowledge involving insights into the depths of truth beyond the intellect
3 *transiency*, that such states are short-lived, usually up to half an hour at the most
4 *passivity*, that the mystic's will is in abeyance during the experience.

As an example of a mystical experience one of the accounts of a respondent in Wallis's survey of Quaker religious experience is very apt:

> During an eight-day silent Zen retreat . . . I was walking alone on an open hillside soon after dawn. Turning my head and looking across the valley I was greatly surprised and amazed to find myself weeping *and* laughing with feelings of tenderness and recognition and a kind of anguish at the marvel of what was happening. The landscape had not changed but I was transformed.
>
> As an artist I am accustomed to seeing things form themselves into beautiful patterns and images; offering themselves as inspirations for painting. This was quite another kind of beauty. I was no longer the observer seeing it. I was at one with it. I was it, and I recognized the experience as though I was remembering it. It aroused me and returned what can only be named love.
>
> It was as though all questions were answered. And the miracle of existence itself was not only revealed but possessed. I looked around at the muddy footpath, the stones on the path. I looked at the clouds and the overcast sky. Everything was ordinary, how it always was, yet everything was transformed – inwardly. Outwardly the same, inwardly a radiance. Personal and impersonal, beyond words. And a thought which was more like a voice said, 'Now I know all is well, I am satisfied and I am happy to die.' (1993; 61–2)

(Mystical experiences are further discussed in Chapter 6 when assessment issues are considered.)

Spiritual, religious or mystical experiences often just happen to people but they can also be sought after. James (1901) reminds us that yoga in its original form is intended to facilitate the experiential union of the individual with the divine and constitutes a form of training for mystical insight or Samadhi; likewise Buddhist meditation. In Islam the Sufis follow a mystical path aiming at union with the divine, often through the use of dance and movement. In Judaism are to be found the Hasidim, a movement of mystically inspired Jews who date back to the early eighteenth century (and who incidentally strongly influenced the theologian and philosopher Martin Buber whose work will be considered in Chapter 2). Within Christianity there have always been individual mystics such as St John of the Cross and Mother Julian of Norwich (who is frequently referred to by Brian Thorne, (1998)). One mystically inclined group that sits uneasily within the Christian tradition are the Quakers founded in the mid-seventeenth century.

Within the therapy world, transpersonal therapists (as explored in Chapter 2) have a particular interest in altered states of consciousness, peak experiences, and work with an awareness of spirituality in the lives of themselves and their clients.

HOW HEALTHY IS SPIRITUALITY?

The exploration of spirituality and spirituality experiences has so far tended to assume that people with active spiritual lives are inevitably psychologically healthy. This is clearly not always the case. Apart from the high profile cases of religious cults that go 'off the rails' (for example the mass suicide at Jonestown, or the FBI seige at Waco), individuals occasionally commit violent and destructive acts while claiming to be following the voice of God. (I will ignore here the shameful part played by organized religions in most major wars across the globe, perhaps epitomized during the English Civil War in the 1640s when both sides would go into battle singing hymns.)

For the religiously minded individual who seeks therapeutic help there may well be clear mental health issues to be addressed, especially at assessment, which are explored in Chapter 6. What I wish to address here in more general terms is: how healthy is the pursuit of an active religious life? Various attempts have been made to distinguish between healthy and unhealthy forms of religiosity and spirituality. One of the most influential was that proposed by Allport who advocated that we can view people's religious position as either immature and extrinsic or mature and intrinsic. People with an extrinsic orientation: 'use religion for their own ends . . . The embraced creed is lightly held or else selectively shaped to fit more primary needs . . . The extrinsic type turns to God, but without turning away from self' (Allport and Ross, 1967: 434). In contrast, the intrinsic 'find their master motive in religion . . . Having embraced a creed the individual endeavors to internalize it and follow it fully. It is in this sense that he lives his religion' (1967: 464).

Richards and Bergin (1997) point out that several abnormal or patho-logical forms of religious experience and behaviour have been described and may appear in the consulting room. These include: 'demonic possession, scrupulosity ("obsessive overconcern for one's sinfulness"), ecstasy or frenzy, repetitive denominational shifting, acedia ("spiritual languor or depres-sion"), glossolalia ("speaking in tongues") . . . sudden conversion, and crisis . . . religious delusions, compulsions, and masochism' (1997: 183, 185).

I will not explore this in great detail here, but Richards and Bergin (1997) do a useful review of the existing research literature especially within the US context. However, the cultural context must be borne in mind. It is dangerously easy to misdiagnose someone from another culture or ethnic group, especially from within a Western Judaeo–Christian viewpoint (further discussed in Chapter 2).

THE LEGACY OF FREUD

It has become commonplace to knock Freud and denigrate his contri-bution to modern therapeutic practice. The fact that he attracts so much criticism can be taken as a sign of the continuing importance and rele-vance of his work. Like it or not, the psychoanalytic and psychodynamic schools of therapy are here to stay and remain one of the leading strands of modern therapeutic thought and practice, in spite of their relative decline in the USA.

We now know that Freud did not get it all right, and indeed he needs to be read from a perspective of his own time and culture, and we should not take everything he said in some kind of fundamentalist, non-critical way. At best Freud had an ambivalent attitude to spirituality and spiritual experi-ences, and his view of religion was even more negative. There are many writers from within the psychoanalytic and psychodynamic traditions who are positive about the spiritual part of our lives (see for instance Foskett and Jacobs, 1989; Frankl, 1947; 1973; 1978; Guntrip, 1956; Herman, 1987; Jung, 1933; 1967; Symington, 1994). However, too many still follow Freud's negative view of religion and it is his view that we will consider here.

Freud clearly linked humankind's need for religion to our early child-hood experiences: 'The derivation of religious needs from the infant's helplessness and the longing for the father aroused by it seems to me incontrovertible' (1963: 9). He saw religion as providing people with a false explanation for the uncertainties of life; it also gave them a bene-volent God, a father figure who could be appealed to in prayer.

In contrast to the answers provided by religion, Freud's own view of the nature of life was much more down to earth: 'the purpose of life is simply the programme of the pleasure principle' (1963: 13). Freud saw this as the striving after happiness, or at the very least avoiding or minimizing suffering. Although religion could have a part to play here, indeed he recognized its potential as a 'crooked cure' (quoted in Hay, 1982), Freud was disparaging about the value of this: 'The whole thing is potentially so infantile, so foreign to reality . . . it is painful to think that the great majority of mortals will never be able to rise above this view of life' (1963: 11).

Freud (1963) was especially dismissive of those philosophers who, as he saw it, fought a 'pitiful rearguard action' to preserve religion. This is in keeping with Freud's view that psychoanalysis was a science, and thereby taking the side of science in opposition to religion as was the case in late Victorian times. His vehemence inevitably led to interpretations as to why he took such a viewpoint. For example, Isbister (1985) and Vitz (1993) link Freud's attack on religion with his unhappy childhood experiences with a Catholic nanny! Freud's Jewish origins and their impact on his theories is discussed in Chapter 2.

With regard to people's claims to have had spiritual experiences, Freud was initially neutral and said, 'I cannot discover this "oceanic" feeling in myself' (1963: 2). This did not lead him to deny such feelings in other people, but he did not see them as the primary root of religious needs. He regarded these oceanic feelings as 'strange', and commented that they 'fit in so badly with the fabric of our psychology' (1963: 2). He suggested such feelings could be traced back to infancy, where the child did not see itself as separate from the world. To Freud, the only non-pathological adult experience of such a loss of boundary occurs when two adults first fall in love.

This points us to the crux of the matter: can we as adults lose our separateness from each other in non-pathological ways other than falling in love? Spiritual experiences may be just that, that is, a non-pathological loss of boundary. People's descriptions of spiritual experiences and the often positive consequences of such experiences (Elkins et al., 1988; Grof and Grof, 1989; Hay, 1982) challenge Freud's view that they are pathological, and it is probably true to say that today many if not most analysts would take a more open view of such experiences. It is very difficult, indeed probably impossible, to completely bracket one's own assumptions and experience of spirituality and religion. However, such experiences are not fading away in our modern world.

Some therapists, reported in a survey in the USA (Allman et al., 1992), view any mystical experience as potentially psychotic, regardless of the information presented. Indeed, one of the fears expressed by many people who report spiritual experiences (Hay, 1982) including the author (West, 1985) is that they will be regarded as insane. Consequently, people tend not to share such experiences.

WHY THERAPISTS NEED TRAINING IN DEALING WITH SPIRITUAL ISSUES

Spirituality, like money, seems to have taken the place of sex as a taboo topic: rather embarrassing, something not to be spoken about, although this is perhaps lessening (Rowan, 1993). However, we know from the work of David Hay mentioned earlier how common religious experiences are; indeed from the work of Allman et al. (1992) we know how frequently mystical experiences occur to clients of psychotherapists in the USA.

Therapists who are dismissive of spirituality when challenged have been known to reply, 'Well, my clients never discuss their spirituality with me.' However, it is commonly accepted that clients will avoid exploring topics that their therapists are 'deaf to', and will somehow pick this up without being told. There is a case to be made for asking a client during the assessment stage whether they follow any spiritual disciplines, or whether they grew up in a religious household (Richards and Bergin, 1997). By so raising the question of spirituality and religion the client is more enabled to speak of it.

Part of the training therapists need is to explore their countertransference responses to spirituality and religion. Many of us suffered in our childhood and later years in response to heavy handed religious teachings and these can lead us to regard all religion and all spirituality as harmful and unnecessary. Lannert (1991) explored the countertransference issues for therapists working in the USA, and found that few therapists had had any training around spirituality and religious issues and relied instead on their own convictions to guide their work with clients. She concluded: 'It is imperative that we, as professionals, monitor our own resistances, countertransference issues, and value systems regarding spiritual and religious issues if we are to meet most ethically and efficaciously the special needs of our clients.'

To spell out in detail what a training programme around spirituality issues for therapists would include would take a book in itself. However, some elements can be sketched in and will be further explored in subsequent chapters. Here are a few suggestions as to what preparation therapists in training and afterwards could usefully consider:

1 Examine their own prejudices and biases around spirituality and religion, both positive and negative.
2 Familiarize themselves with some of the literature around spiritual experiences (e.g. Hay, 1982; James, 1901) and pastoral therapy and spiritual direction (Jeff, 1987; Leech, 1994; Lyall, 1995).
3 Explore a religion from a different culture than their own including attending a religious service (see Lee and Amstrong, 1995).
4 Address the assessment issues involved, including when a spiritual experience might have psychotic elements to it, when a client needs a spiritual referral and whom to refer the client on to, and the part played by spiritual emergence and spiritual emergency in some people's spiritual development (Grof and Grof, 1989; Lukoff, 1985).
5 Develop a sense of some of the main maps and theories of spiritual development, those of Wilber in particular.

6   Study implicit and explicit spiritual forms of counselling (e.g. Jung, 1933; Richards and Bergin, 1997; Rowan, 1993; Thorne, 1991; 1998).
7   Clarify the differences and overlaps between spiritual direction, pastoral care and counselling or psychotherapy (Leech, 1994; Lyall, 1995), including non-Christian forms of spiritual care (Vigne, 1991).
8   Be engaged in their own form of spiritual development as recommended by Rowan (1993).
9   Have appropriate supervision arrangements in place.

THE DECLINE OF CHRISTIANITY AND CONVENTIONAL RELIGION

Although claims of revival in church attendance are often made, the more conventional parts of the Christian Churches have increasingly elderly congregations. Newer, and often evangelical, and sometimes more fundamentalist Churches are growing in size. The picture is less clear for non-Christian religions in Britain, but the trend of a decline in mainstream approaches coupled with an increase in innovative and/or fundamentalist approaches also features. Also increasing is what has been disparagingly referred to as 'do-it-yourself' or 'New Age Spirituality' in which people pursue their spiritual interests outside conventional religious frameworks. It is difficult to put a figure to the numbers that are pursuing New Age Spirituality but it is a group that overlaps with the therapy world, especially with humanistic and transpersonal therapies.

Two fascinating facts can be placed alongside this decline in conventional religious attendance. Firstly, it has no apparent impact on the number of people having spiritual experiences (as explored earlier in the light of Hay, 1982). Secondly, Halmos (1965) in Britain, and Nelson and Torrey (1973) in the USA, have pointed out how strikingly the decline in clergy and other church workers has been paralleled by an equivalent increase in social workers and therapists. They speculate that people are now seeking help from secular therapists where in the past they sought it from the Church. They may be exaggerating how great was the therapeutic part played by the Christian Churches but it does raise questions about the role of therapists in our society, and whether there is a spiritual need behind at least some of the requests for therapy which is not always being brought to light.

THE SPLIT BETWEEN SCIENCE AND RELIGION

A rigid religious system has trouble with creative people, be they scientists or artists. Inevitably the authoritarian Catholic Church was challenged by early scientists including Galileo. To develop, modern science had to be free of Church control. In the so-called Age of Enlightenment it seemed that science was the inevitable enemy of religion and would eventually surpass it. Such confidence is less frequently expressed today. Religions in some cases have at least partially caught up with modern scientific thinking, and in the twentieth century of world wars and the Holocaust there is less confidence expressed in science as a solution to human problems.

There are, in addition, growing signs of something of a *rapprochement* between religion and science, helped perhaps by the tangle into which modern physics has got itself in trying to make sense of subatomic particles and energies. Various scientists (Capra, 1982; Sheldrake, 1994) have explored the increasing overlap between modern physics and current and ancient religious views of the cosmos. The concept of Gaia, of the earth as a living entity, has developed as an expression of the interdependence of all life on our planet, and for many people this energetic ecological reality is experienced as deeply spiritual (Lovelock, 1979).

SHAMANISM

The modern psychotherapist . . . relies to a large extent on the same psychological mechanisms used by the faith healer, shaman, physician, priest, and others, and the results, as reflected by the evidence of therapeutic outcomes, appear to be substantially similar. (Strupp, 1972: 277)

What is generally not considered, however, is that the indigenous services offered by traditional practitioners have effectively addressed physical and mental illness for millennia. (Lee and Armstrong, 1995: 444)

The concept of Gaia, of the earth as a living being, would not be seen as alien by many shamans. Shamanism has become an area of great interest in recent years with shamanic practices increasingly being offered on workshops or in individual consultations within Britain. Shamanism has been historically viewed as a practice within aboriginal or so-called primitive societies but many commentators have recognized similar practices within modern societies and within psychotherapy, as will be discussed below. In addition a number of therapists, many of a humanistic persuasion, are now explicitly introducing elements from shamanism into their therapeutic practice.

Eliade did some of the earliest anthropological research into shamanism and provides us with a useful definition: 'A first definition of this complex phenomenon, and perhaps the least hazardous, will be shamanism = techniques of ecstasy' (1964: 4). Here 'ecstasy' is being used in the sense of being taken out of one's ordinary state of awareness. Eliade adds: 'the shaman specializes in a trance during which his soul is believed to leave his body and ascend to the sky or descend to the underworld' (1964: 5).

This journeying by the soul of the shaman often involves contact with spirits, sometimes of a dangerous nature, as part of a healing ritual for the client. The cosmos of the shaman consists of three realms: the upper world of the Gods; the middle world of material reality; and the lower world, the place of the dead and of wisdom (Bates, 1993; Pendzik, 1988).

Bates (1993) points out the similarities that exist between the shamanic views of reality presented in different 'primitive' cultures around the world. He believes that shamanism is unlikely to have descended from one central prehistoric source, and that it represents something shared, something common to all human reality. Winkleman suggests that 'the trance-based aspects of shamanistic practice are universal' (1989: 18). Nevertheless, he presents an evolutionary model for healers that differentiates shamans in hunter-gatherer societies from what he calls shaman/healers in agricultural societies and mediums or healers in industrial societies. However, his model does not account for the huge increase in shamanic practices in the United States, Britain and elsewhere. Perhaps this model needs to be extended to include the postmodern or post-industrial society?

Eliade (1964) says that mystics, unlike shamans, do not necessarily make soul journeys. He also differentiates shamans and mystics from those suffering from mental illness. Many observers fall into the trap of viewing shamans as mentally ill (for further discussion see Grof and Grof, 1986; 1989; Walsh, 1989; 1994; Watson, 1994). The question of appropriate diagnosis and treatment of clients with troubling forms of spiritual experience is discussed in Chapter 6.

Although shamans and shamanism are traditionally regarded as being part of primitive tribal culture, various writers are now noting similar experiences occurring in Western societies (Grof and Grof, 1989; Walsh, 1994; Willis 1992a; 1992b). Willis (1992b) records that out of 20 new healers meeting on a training course in Scotland, 19 had had either a serious illness or an accident in the year prior to their emergence as healers. He talks of the 'catastrophic' impact of their illnesses, which reminded him of his anthropological fieldwork in Zambia with tribal shamans. Willis comments that although such experiences are expected for tribal healers, in Western society similar traditions do not exist.

Ellenberger (1970) draws our attention to the significance of the initiatory or creative illness suffered by shamans, and claims that both Freud and Jung had similar experiences. He describes this creative illness as being a 'severe neurosis or psychosis' that may last several years. When the subject emerges from it, he or she is convinced that they have discovered a universal truth. Followers of either a shaman or an analyst have to undergo a similar initiation, whether it takes the form of a training analysis or a shamanic initiation.

Pietroni from a medical context says that the shaman is found in almost all cultures and is the 'primogenitor of all subsequent health-care practitioners' (1993: 303). Pietroni (1993) and Ellenberger (1970) comment on the number of psychotherapy techniques developed this century which have their counterparts in shamanistic practices.

Peters and Price-Williams (1980), in an experiential analysis of shamanism, link shamanic flight and its therapeutic value with modern psychotherapies that use dream analysis. They comment on the similarity between the shaman's trance states and certain psychotherapy techniques. (A similar point is made by Eliade, 1960 and by the Jungian analyst Greenleaf, 1978.). They also compare the dissociative element in shamanism with the psychodrama of Moreno (1947) and with Perls's Gestalt therapy (1969a; 1969b) and conclude that: 'it is impossible to take an absolute position regarding the authenticity of shamanic trance' (Peters and Price-Williams, 1980: 401).

Pendzik (1988) points out the overlaps between drama therapy and shamanism, and compares the three regions of the shamanic universe – the lower, middle, and upper worlds – with Assagioli's three levels of the personal unconscious, and concludes that the two share a similar model.

In a novel development the anthropologist Goodman (1986) describes how she used rhythmic drumming and body postures derived from shamanistic practices to achieve shamanistic-like experiences outside religious and cultural frameworks, and succeeded. This suggests that shamanic experiences are not restricted to 'primitive' culture, and that under the right conditions many people can achieve altered states of consciousness akin to those of the shaman. There may however be dangers of mental disturbances in exploring this territory without due care.

Inevitably shamanistic techniques have become something to be sought out, learnt and then taught by Western people interested in psychotherapy and healing. This has often been accomplished by contact with American Indians and other native or aboriginal people, and workshops in their therapeutic techniques are increasingly popular in the USA and more recently in Britain. For some people such approaches seem to be fulfilling a need for a non-Christian experientially based form of spirituality rooted in nature. It appears to some commentators that psychotherapy has gone full circle and is once more returning to its spiritual roots in shamanic practices (Krippner, 1992; Pietroni, 1993).

In the context of traditional healing it is worth recalling that the ancient pre-Christian beliefs of the people of Britain was paganism. Paganism, rather confusing described as a new religious movement by Barker (1989), is currently enjoying something of a revival and is claimed to be the fastest growing religion in Britain (Seymour, 1998). Paganism has a number of healing rituals within its religious practice and deserves serious study free of the negative image it has been given by many Christians. Seymour (1998) suggests that given its increasing popularity it deserves such an approach within therapist training courses.

In this chapter we have considered what spirituality is and have acknowledged the significance of religious, spiritual and mystical experiences including their relevance for modern psychotherapy. The training issues that arise have been noted. Freud's negative legacy to those seeking to include a healthy concept of spirituality within psychotherapy has been noted, together with a recognition of the decline in Britain of the mainstream Christian Churches, and the historical antagonism between science and religion. Shamanism has been explored in passing as a possible link with aboriginal forms of therapy and healing that overlap with many modern-day psychotherapeutic practices, especially those of a humanistic nature, and its link with New Age Spirituality is noted. Subsequent chapters take up many of these themes and related issues in greater detail, exploring their relevance to the practice of counselling and psychotherapy.

2

Therapy and Spirituality

> Ever since the birth of modern psychology souls have been out of fashion. (Edwards, 1992)

> The products of meditation are insight, awareness, equanimity and magnamity, and any therapist who declines to undertake a practice that strengthens and expands these vital therapeutic qualities has some explaining to do. (Claxton, 1996: 320)

It is apparent from the brief survey in Chapter 1 that spirituality is an important part of many people's lives and that it has a significant impact on personal health and well-being. As a result it might be expected to be part, perhaps an important part, of counselling and psychotherapy. Indeed, counselling and psychotherapy have spiritual origins to be found in practices of witches, priests and shamans (Benner, 1988; Ellenberger, 1970; Healey, 1993; McLeod, 1993; 1998; Pietroni, 1993). The word 'psychotherapist' is derived from the Greek words *psyche* meaning soul or breath of life, and *therapeia* denoting attendant or servant. 'Psychotherapist' therefore literally means servant or attender of the soul (Tick, 1992).

In Britain prior to the Industrial Revolution, individual problems in living were primarily dealt with from a religious perspective in the local community. This could include the so-called 'cure of souls' by the local priest (McNeill, 1951). Gradually, as people were drawn off the land and into the growing cities to work in factories, there was a shift away from tolerating disturbed behaviour within the local community to the emergence of mental asylums, beginning in the middle of the eighteenth century. Some of the early asylums were run on religious lines including those run by Quakers, notably by Tuke in York who pioneered an approach called moral treatment. However, conditions in many of the asylums were appalling, including Bethlem Hospital where the antics of the inmates could be watched as a public spectacle.

Various Acts of Parliament in the mid nineteenth century gave control over mental health to the medical profession (Lunacy Act 1842, General Medical Act 1858). Emotional and behavioural problems had thus become medicalized; the new services were controlled by men and used to oppress women (McLeod, 1998); there was now a 'trade in lunacy'; and medical science had replaced religion as the main framework for understanding madness. Szasz (1988) comments how the repression of 'heretic-madman' was transferred from the priest to the psychiatrist. By the end of the nineteenth century psychiatry had a dominant position in the care of the insane, now regarded as 'mentally ill'. From within medicine and psychiatry arose the new specialism of psychotherapy. By the turn of the century Freud had already published his key book *The Interpretation of Dreams*.

If the nineteenth century was the time when the care of those mentally ill was taken away from the Church and others, and given to the medical professional, the twentieth century has increasingly seen how people with problems in living are cared for by psychotherapists and counsellors rather than by the Church, family or local community. Halmos in his seminal book *The Faith of the Counsellors* (1965) contrasts the decline in clergy and other religious employees with a rise in medical and psychological solutions to people's problems, with a corresponding increase in the number of people offering counselling. (Nelson and Torrey, 1973, present a similar picture for developments in the USA.) However, the influence of Christianity and the Christian Church is apparent in the origins of a number of agencies which offer therapy and befriending including Relate, Westminster Pastoral Foundation, Alcoholics Anonymous, Samaritans and Cruse. The Association for Pastoral Care and Counselling, formed in 1970 by mainly Christian clergy and some Jewish associates, was one of the founding groups of the British Association for Counselling and remains an active group within the counselling world, providing an alternative voice to secular counselling.

However, the secular nature of psychotherapy and counselling continues apace. Indeed, sending in the counsellors has become almost a knee-jerk reaction to any crisis or disaster occurring in Britain, with few questioning the appropriateness of such actions. (Some notable challenges to this orthodoxy include Howard, 1995 and Smail, 1987.) To rub salt into the wound, 'therapyspeak' seems to have quite a currency within the Christian Church: indeed some of the dilemmas about religious faith and belief appear to be masked by the use of comfortable words borrowed from the therapeutic encounter. Hurding (1985) and others have warned against such conflation.

FREUD AND JUNG

Despite these spiritual antecedents, counselling and psychotherapy continue to have an uneasy relationship with spirituality. Many modern-day, largely secular therapists tend to ignore spirituality, or see it in terms of regression, as something for the client to grow out of. In this respect such therapists are following the lead of Freud, whose views were briefly explored in Chapter 1. However, although Freud's view of religion and spirituality dominated the world of psychoanalysis, even in the early days there was a counter-viewpoint expressed by Carl Jung. Jung viewed religion not in terms of creeds but in terms of experience: 'The term "religion" designates the attitude peculiar to a consciousness which has been changed by experience of the numinosum' (1958: 8).

'Numinosum' was a term Jung took from Otto, which he defined as: 'a dynamic agency or effect not caused by an arbitrary act of will' (1958: 7). Jung saw the practice of being religious as intended to produce changes through numinous experiences, and according to Levy: 'Both Jungians and transpersonal psychologists view the experience of the numinous as intrinsically therapeutic' (1983: 47).

Although Jung regarded organized religion as being founded on such numinous or spiritual experiences, he questioned whether such experiences were available to churchgoers in modern times. Jung recognized the psychic reality of the spiritual or religious need in all of humankind and stated: 'A psychoneurosis must be understood ultimately as the suffering of a soul which has not discovered its meaning' (1958: 330–1). Jung was convinced that our neuroses had present as well as past causes, otherwise, he insisted, they would cease to be active. Consequently he regarded 'the religious problem which the patient puts before me as authentic and as possible causes of the neurosis' (1958: 333).

Thus, in contrast to Freud, Jung saw spirituality and spiritual experiences as potentially healthy aspects of our being. He is often quoted as saying: 'Among my patients in the second half of life – that is over 35 years of age – there has not been a single one whose problem has not been in the last resort that of finding a religious outlook on life' (1933: 164).

Jung, however, has his critics. Symington (1994) criticizes Jung for advocating that we submit to the power of the numinosum (which could be seen to parallel the spiritual notion of surrender to the divine). Symington argues that such submission is in fact to a savage superego rather than some spiritual external agency. He insists that such submission will keep the person at the infantile stage of development.

From a transpersonal perspective, John Rowan (1993) criticizes Jung for reducing everything to psychology and thereby having to cram everything spiritual into the collective unconscious. Nevertheless Jung was an early pioneer of an analytic approach that included religion and spirituality. On the archway leading to his front door Jung had carved the Latin inscription 'Vocatus atque non vocatus, deus aderit', which translates as 'Whether he is called or not, the God will be present' (quoted in West, 1983). Jung had a huge impact on therapeutic approaches which honoured the spiritual, especially on the emergence of transpersonal therapy.

Despite the work of Jung there remain profound difficulties in an acceptance of the healthy part that spirituality can play in people's lives within the analytic community. Indeed Payne et al., when discussing this issue, state: 'the separation, if not opposition, between psychoanalysis and religion is the essence of the naturalistic explanations of psychoanalysis. Religion is nonadmissible given its assumptions of transcendence and theology' (1992: 176).

There are other writers within the analytic world who are accepting of the healthy part that spirituality and spiritual experiences play within human lives. For example Lovinger (1984) relates object relations to religious development and beliefs, and insists that there are important therapeutic data to be found in our clients' religious imagery, echoing the earlier work of Guntrip (1956). Shafranske (1988) also draws on object relations theory as an aid to understanding unconscious elements in religious experiences. A psychodynamic approach to pastoral counselling has been developed in which clients' stories are interpreted in terms of religious stories and teachings (Foskett and Jacobs, 1989; Foskett and Lyall, 1988).

Turning to what may be deemed spiritual phenomena or spiritual experiences within the therapeutic relationship, Elizabeth Mintz believes that transpersonal forces are the only adequate explanation for some events that occur in psychotherapy. Furthermore she maintains that her use of the word 'transpersonal' 'implies recognition of cosmic energy-forces, which may or may not be seen in a religious or spiritual perspective' (1978: 90).

Mollon is of the opinion that the subtle energy system of our bodies, or the human aura or energy field, is the 'unconscious source of counter-transference material' (1991: 16). In other words, psychic or intuitive insights are available to the therapist via his or her subtle energy field. Mollon regards 'psychotherapy and psychoanalysis as just vehicles for healing' (personal communication, 1992).

A number of writers have written at length about psychic, intuitive and paranormal implications within the analytic relationship (see Coleman, 1958; Ehrenwald, 1954; Tornatore and Tornatore, 1977) which I have further discussed elsewhere (West, 1995a).

Perhaps when the energy fields of therapist and client are well connected there is both a clear channel for empathic and intuitive information and the possibility of more profound experiences occurring that would be seen by one or both participants as spiritual. The Jungian analyst Hall (1984) refers to a 'transformative field' in his description of transference and countertransference phenomena, occurring when both parties (i.e. therapist and client) are deeply involved and may be transformed by the interactions. This links in with Buber's (1970) talk of the in-between, that is, what lies or comes into being between two people in an I–Thou relationship.

The world of therapy today is often divided into four different broad waves, although this omits distinctly Christian and other religiously influenced forms of therapy which are considered later in this chapter. The four waves are seen as beginning with Freud and psychoanalysis around 1900; followed from around 1920 by behavioural and latterly cognitive-behavioural; by humanistic approaches from around 1940; and finally transpersonal around 1960. Since then it could be argued that a fifth wave exists in systemic approaches (Cumming, personal communication, 1994); or that the fifth wave comprises eclectic and integrative approaches

(Hollanders, 1997; Norcross and Dryden, 1990); or that multicultural therapy forms the next wave or can be considered as the fourth wave (Ponterotto et al., 1995).

COGNITIVE BEHAVIOURISM

Behaviour therapy arose in contrast to psychoanalysis and regarded people's problems in living as learnt and therefore capable of being unlearnt. Its focus was on observable human behaviour and how to change it rather than on internal processes such as dreams, fantasies and impulses. It could be said that cognitive-behavioural approaches to therapy have little to say on the topic of spirituality (Rowan, 1993). However, some recent developments have occurred in which use of cognitive-behavioural treatments with religious contents have met with some success with religiously orientated clients (Payne et al., 1992). This has not depended on the spiritual view-point of the therapist: indeed in one study (Propst et al., 1992) that used theological reflections based on scriptural passages and imagery work, therapists without a religious viewpoint have produced better outcomes in their clients than those religiously inclined! The same study of groupwork with depressed clients also included both a control group and a pastoral counselling group. The pastoral counselling group produced outcomes for the group members that were equal to or greater than those of the professionally conducted cognitive-behavioural therapy. Propst et al. con-cluded that: 'if replicated this has significant public health implications because a large portion of the public is religiously oriented and there are far more pastors than therapists'.

Marsha Linehan (Linehan and Schmidt, 1995) has integrated the use of Zen Buddhism and behavioural therapy in the treatment of clients with borderline personality disorders. There are possibilities for using behav-ioural techniques within a Buddhist framework and vice versa: indeed, 'Buddhism has much in common with the behavioural tradition of therapy' (de Silva, 1996: 231).

HUMANISTIC THERAPY

Humanistic-existential thinking lends itself to religiously based issues . . . we are long on theory and short on evidence. (Payne et al., 1992)

Within the humanistic tradition the issue of spirituality and how it is worked with therapeutically varies between therapists and between schools. Humanistic therapists are more willing than psychoanalysts to acknowledge the possible health in a client's spirituality and they are less likely to interpret mystical experiences in terms of the client's regression (Allman et al., 1992).

Most humanistic therapists operate from a holistic model which sees people as physical, emotional, mental and spiritual beings. Consequently spirituality and spiritual experiences will tend to be tolerated and perhaps even welcomed as phenomena to be explored, but the traditional human-istic therapist is less likely to be experienced in working with such phenomena than the transpersonal therapist. Whilst the training pro-grammes of humanistic therapists may touch on the spiritual and the transpersonal, this will not tend to be in any systematic, worked-out way. Consequently the response to the client's spirituality will usually depend on the individual practitioner (Rowan, 1993).

Because the humanistic mindset is by nature open to exploring unusual phenomena, in contrast to the more dogmatic analytic approach, those writing about the spiritual from a humanistic point of view tend to adopt a positive or otherwise neutral stance. For example, one of the key founders of humanistic therapy was Carl Rogers. After an early religious upbringing that culminated in entry into a seminary to train as a priest, Rogers turned his back on religion. However, towards the end of his life he identified a new spiritual dimension in his work, and added to his long-established core conditions for effective counselling (unconditional positive regard, congruence and empathy) a further quality which he had observed in himself and other experienced counsellors (Kirschenbaum and Henderson, 1990a). He called this *presence*:

> I find that when I am closer to my inner, intuitive self, when I am somehow in touch with the unknown in me, when perhaps I am in a slightly altered state of consciousness in the relationship, then whatever I do seems to be full of healing. Then simply my *presence* is releasing and helpful . . . I may behave in strange and impulsive ways in the relationship, ways which I cannot justify rationally, which have nothing to do with my thought processes . . . At these moments it seems that my inner spirit has reached out and touched the inner spirit of the other . . . Profound growth and healing energies are present. (Rogers in Kirschenbaum and Henderson, 1990a: 137)

Rogers is describing the conditions that he feels make presence possible. However, presence is still a source of controversy in the person-centred world (McLeod, 1993; Van Belle, 1990). Van Belle is critical of what he regards as Rogers becoming increasingly 'preoccupied with a mystical, spiritual world full of psychic phenomena' (1990: 52). He also criticizes Rogers for not providing clear guidelines for such work, because he does not tell us 'what new things a therapist must do to facilitate this mystical transpersonal experience in clients' (1990: 54).

I cannot help but feel sympathy for Van Belle's view since it coincides with my own initial reaction to a first reading of Rogers's view of presence. I was excited by his description of a phenomenon that was familiar to me from the world of spiritual healing (West, 1985) but also angry since Rogers appeared to me to have driven a coach and horses through his

elegantly constructed theory of the core conditions as necessary and sufficient (Rogers, 1951). The core conditions were at least relatively easy to
research, teach and measure. But how to do the same with 'acting in ways
which I cannot logically justify' (Kirschenbaum and Henderson, 1990a:
137)?

Mearns (1994) perhaps provides us with a way out of this dilemma. He
suggests that presence can be referred to without using mystical language
and can be understood within existing concepts like a blending of the core
conditions together with a counsellor's ability to be truly still within him/
herself. However, removing the mysticism from Rogers's discussion of
presence also helps to keep counselling separate from spirituality.

Other counsellors and psychotherapists have noticed similar developments: indeed increasing numbers of humanistic therapists (and those of
other orientations) appear to move towards a more mystical and spiritual
view of life as they get older (see for instance Heron, 1992; Reich, 1969;
Rogers, 1980; Rowan, 1993). Nor is it exclusive to men (Chaplin, 1989;
Edwards, 1992). This could be an unconscious following of the Hindu
tradition of the second half of one's life being devoted more to the
spiritual, what Ken Wilber (1980) and Frances Vaughan (1986) speak of as
the 'inward arc'.

The practice of humanistic therapy is seen by some as being akin to the
Buddhist practice of mindfulness (Tart and Deikman, 1991). That is, by
listening closely and being aware of one's client and of how one is affected
by them, one is being mindful. Such awareness is what Freud called 'free
floating attention' although he did not regard it as spiritual. However,
when practised for many hours a week it could be seen as a spiritual
practice resulting in spiritual fruits, which is discussed further in Chapter 3.

Contrast this notion of a healthy spiritual practice within therapy with
the oft quoted paper by the analyst Alexander (1931). This held that the
end result of Buddhist spiritual practice is a regressed state resembling
catatonia, which shows how symptoms of behaviour taken out of context
can be easily misunderstood.

Watts (1961) comments on the parallel between Rogers's non-directive
therapy and the philosophy of Taoism which perhaps resulted from Rogers's
visit to China while he was young (Kirschenbaum and Henderson, 1990a).
The influence of Eastern spirituality on Gestalt therapy has also been clearly
acknowledged (Clarkson, 1989).

Another example of a person-centred therapist clearly embracing
spirituality is provided by Brian Thorne. Thorne describes a quality of
'tenderness' which is akin to Rogers's presence (Thorne, 1991; Mearns
and Thorne, 1988). He states that he no longer has to 'leave my eternal
soul outside the door' of the counselling room, and that he can now
'capitalize on many hours spent in prayer and worship' (1988: 37). He is
bold enough to state that: 'The future of the person-centred approach may
well depend on its capacity to embrace the world of spiritual reality'
(1991: 127).

A similar viewpoint is to be found in the philosophical writings of Buber (1970), in the existential work of Maurice Friedman (1993) and others with dialogical therapy in the USA, and Victor Frankl's *The Doctor and the Soul: from Psychotherapy to Logotherapy* (1973). Martin Buber (1878–1965), the Jewish philosopher and mystic, has had a profound impact on many therapists especially those of a humanistic or an existentialist inclination. Buber maintained that there are two types of relationship: the I–It relationship in which one treats the other as different from oneself, as something of an object, and the I–Thou relationship in which the other is related to as kin. Within an I–Thou relationship an energetic meeting between the two people becomes possible. In such a meeting, according to Buber, God is to be found. Buber also said that even in the best relationship we move between I–It and I–Thou.

Buber's writing has an arresting poetic style, as if he is inviting us to move out of the rational logical part of our being and to have something of an I–Thou relationship with his words: 'There is no I taken in itself, but only the I of the primary word I–Thou and the I of the primary word I–It . . . If I face a human being as my Thou, and say the primary word I–Thou to him, he is not a thing among things, and does not consist of things' (1970: 24).

A number of therapists, including Rogers and more recently Clarkson (1990), maintain that they experience something akin to an I–Thou relationship with their clients. Buber was sceptical about this and in a famous dialogue with Carl Rogers (Kirschenbaum and Henderson, 1990b) took him to task over the power inherent within the therapy relationship. Parts of the dialogue went as follows:

> *Rogers*: I have wondered whether your concept of what you have termed the I–Thou relationship is similar to what I see as the effective moments in a therapeutic relationship? [*Rogers then presents his views of the therapeutic relationship in terms of his core conditions.*] Now, I see that as having some resemblance to the sort of thing you have talked about in the I–Thou relationship. Yet I suspect there are differences . . .
>
> *Buber*: A man coming to you for help. The essential difference between your role in this situation and his is obvious. He comes for help to you. You don't come for help to him. And not only this, but you are able, more or less, to help him. He can do different things to you but not help you . . . he is floundering around, he comes to you . . . You are not equals and cannot be.

Rogers, while accepting and agreeing with what Buber says about the objective situation, goes on to insist that the therapeutic relationship is: something immediate, equal, a meeting of two persons on an equal basis – even though in the world of I–It, it could be seen as a very unequal relationship.

> *Buber*: Now Dr Rogers, this is the first point where we must say to one another, 'We disagree.'
>
> *Rogers*: OK. (1990b: 47–52)

Colin Feltham makes clear the difference between Buber's I–Thou and the generality of the therapeutic relationship:

> For Buber, the I–Thou encounter paralleled encounter with God, and is associated with presence and grace rather than with intention, prescription and non-egalitarian helping relationships. This kind of encounter has nothing to do with the therapeutic use of 'immediacy' or the self-conscious development of genuineness. Buber refers to the importance of 'the in-between' and 'the primally simple fact of encounter'. None of this is predictable or exploitable, even for benevolent ends. When it is healing, it is so by grace rather than by design. (1995: 32)

Nevertheless, something akin to I–Thou certainly is claimed and does appear to be happening to a number of therapists. I–Thou relating also seems similar, if not identical, to Rogers's concept of 'presence' (Kirschenbaum and Henderson, 1990a) discussed below, and likewise Thorne's (1991) 'tenderness'.

A further point is worth making. Clarkson (1990) maintains that a better translation for I–Thou is I–You but others disagree. Colin Purcell-Lee (1999) takes a very critical view of Clarkson's understanding of the I–Thou encounter and emphasizes that according to Buber the I–Thou relationship cannot be willed or deployed but occurs through grace, springing from the relationship itself. Purcell-Lee (1999) insists that the use of 'thou' implies a spiritual relationship. There is a tradition of the use of 'thee' and 'thou', including its usage until recent time by British and American Quakers as a more personal style of address, in contrast to 'you' which can be either singular or plural and has a more separate quality.

The other point worth bearing in mind is that there are not degrees of I–Thou, nor can it be taught. Indeed, Buber insists it can barely be talked about, since to talk about it is not to be in it. This is a similar point to that made by Taoist philosophers and by Ken Wilber when talking of spirituality (see Chapter 4). As Buber says:

> The primary word I–Thou can be spoken only with the whole being. Concentration and fusion into the whole being can never take place through my agency, nor can it ever take place without me. I become through my relation to the Thou, as I become I, I say Thou. All real living is meeting. (1970: 24–5)

During a research interview with a Gestalt therapist as part of my research into therapy and healing (West, 1995a; 1997) he spoke of his experience of what he regarded as I–Thou relationships with his clients:

> when the I–Thou relationship is actually functioning then there is some kind of other dimension to the relationship and contact . . . It's ever changing. I mean each moment in time is unique . . . So it is difficult to put into structured words other than to say that one of the factors is a sense of absorption with the client, with the process. Like that's how children become very absorbed with things . . . I would be very alert, or very aware, very attuned with the client, very empathic with their feelings, very quick to sense what they're feeling, sometimes maybe even quicker than them.

I later asked this respondent whether, when in this I–Thou state with his clients, he experienced himself as separate from them or in some sort of common field. His telling reply was:

> Both are true . . . I think there is a sense in the I–Thou in which we are one, yet there's also a sense in which we are still separate . . . I think it may be a problem where we're trying to use language to define things that aren't easily defined. For me anyway, there's a sense of joinedness, of absorption with the client, but also a sense of still being grounded and being separate.

This therapist described his experience of the I–Thou contact as 'like a dance'. His statement about the problem of using language to define things that are not easily defined is valuable. Wilber (1979a) among others (Boucouvalas, 1980; Rowan, 1983; Vaughan, 1989) maintains that there are levels of experience beyond words which words have only a limited capacity to grasp. However, Rowan (1993) and Wilber (1979b) also both insist that not all spiritual experiences are of the same kind and level. Wilber (1979b) presents a very structured 10 stages or levels of spiritual development that human beings can occupy (discussed further in Chapter 6).

TRANSPERSONAL PSYCHOLOGY

Transpersonal psychology is often seen as an offshoot of humanistic psychology, but deserves to be seen as a unique psychology in its own right: 'Transpersonal approaches draw upon the first three forces while going beyond to see humans as intuitive, mystical, psychic, and spiritual. Above all, humans are viewed as unifiable, having the potential for harmonious and holistic development of all their potentials' (Hendricks and Weinhold, 1982: 8).

Jung was the first person to use the word 'transpersonal' with reference to the collective unconscious, and it initially appeared in the phrase 'transpersonal psychology' in the title of the journal of the same name which first appeared in 1969 (Guest, 1989). Sutich, one of the founders of the journal and with Maslow of the Association for Transpersonal Psychology, once said that the word 'transpersonal' was indefinable and should remain so (Hendricks and Weinhold, 1982).

Maslow described transpersonal psychology as 'dealing with transcendent experiences and with transcendent values' (Guest, 1989: 62). Transpersonal psychology is a blanket term that embraces a number of approaches (Boucouvalas, 1980; Guest, 1989) that are able and indeed encourage clients to contact their 'Higher Selves' (Assagioli's term for the soul). Transpersonal psychology draws on elements from psychosynthesis, Jung's analytic psychology, and (according to Boorstein, 1986) ideas and techniques from meditation, chakras, dreamwork, imagery, healing, Sufism, Buddhism, astrology, and after-death experiences.

Grof defined transpersonal experience as 'an experience involving an expansion or extension of consciousness beyond the usual ego boundaries and the limitations of time and space' (1972: 48–9). Vaughan presents us with a definition of transpersonal psychology that underlines its healing nature, when she states it is 'concerned with experiences and aspirations that lead people to seek transcendence, as well as the healing potential of self-transcendence' (1986: 39).

One of the key thinkers of the transpersonal is Ken Wilber (not without his critics, who include Heron, 1992, 1998 and Washburn, 1990) whose spectrum of consciousness model will be considered in some detail in Chapter 6. Wilber's model brings together both Western psychotherapy and Eastern forms of self-development. Transpersonal approaches therefore cover the usual issues of living dealt with by secular Western therapy, but also address spiritual issues.

Wilber suggests that beyond the stage of body–mind integration which he regards as the highest development reached by secular Western therapy, the spiritual realm can be experienced. He divides this realm into three levels which he calls psychic, subtle and causal. Beyond these levels is the ultimate level, Atman, which Wilber insists includes all experience. Wilber (1983) also maintains that we can develop to a point where we are actually at such a level rather than merely 'peeking' at it. He suggests that if this is true, we can investigate the various levels in more depth.

Not all spiritual experiences are wholly healthy. Wilber (1983) insists that we must distinguish between 'authentic spiritual experience' and abnormal or pathological states, a point also made by Grof and Grof (1986; 1989), Assagioli (1986) and Lukoff (1985). Lukoff (1985) goes further and argues for a diagnostic category of mystical experiences with psychotic features. He provides a clear basis for making such a judgement as well as suggestions for a treatment programme. These issues are further explored in Chapter 6. However, it is not the role of the transpersonal therapist to deny that the client's spiritual experience is genuine. That experience is for the client to work with and make sense of. There are relatively few transpersonal therapists in the UK, and it is still regarded very much as an innovative therapy (Jones, 1994). However, transpersonal approaches have had quite an impact on the therapy and healing world. Transpersonal techniques and theories have spread by diffusion and are to be found in complementary medicine and in New Age Spirituality. Some transpersonal approaches like guided fantasy and creative visualization have been widely adopted.

ECLECTIC AND INTEGRATIVE APPROACHES

On the face of it, it would be expected that eclectic and integrative approaches offer the best prospect for integrating spirituality into therapy. Certainly reading Payne et al. (1992) would lead one to such a conclusion.

Clarkson's (1990) five-level therapeutic relationship model is also an integrative one that includes the transpersonal. However, a key focus of much eclecticism and integration is that of brief therapy which is likely to reduce the opportunity to carefully consider spiritual matters, though the first two of my case examples presented in Chapter 7 both involved fewer than seven therapy sessions.

One of the difficulties in working as an eclectic or integrative therapist is in choosing what philosophical base to integrate around. Egan (1990) for example insists on the humanistic nature of his basic philosophy (despite his Jesuit background). Within such a framework specific techniques drawn from religious sources could be used akin to that described earlier under cognitive-behavioural. Nevertheless Egan's basic textbook *The Skilled Helper* makes no reference to spirituality or religion in its index.

Currently eclectic and integrative approaches to therapy remain relatively under-researched compared with the first three waves of therapy schools. However, with the development of a professional body, the Society for Psychotherapy Integration, and the accompanying journal, the picture looks set to change.

MULTICULTURAL THERAPY

Multicultural counseling is counseling that takes place between or among people from different cultural backgrounds. (Jackson, 1995: 3)

Multicultural counseling has been a major source of diversity. Recently, however, it has been recognized that multicultural counseling is generic in nature and therefore that all counseling is multicultural. Thus multiculturalism has joined the movement toward a universal system of counseling. (Patterson, 1996: 227)

One of the questions deserving attention is why different therapies emerge and thrive in different places, cultures and times. Along with this question might go the question of whether therapies are more localized than we realize, and whether they are sometimes applied unhelpfully beyond their time and place. (Feltham, 1995: 66)

According to John McLeod in his seminal work *Introduction to Counselling* (1998), multicultural counselling does not fit easily into the mainstream counselling approaches. Some multicultural counsellors do fall within pure psychodynamic, humanistic or cognitive-behaviour schools but others are more eclectic or integrative. He concludes: 'Multicultural counselling is an integrative approach which uses a culture-based theory of personal identity as a basis for selecting counselling ideas and techniques' (1998: 175).

Multicultural counselling then assumes that membership of a culture or cultures is one of the main influences on the development of individual identity and that a person's problems need to be understood within the light of their culture and its view of health and well-being. This leads us immediately into a discussion of what culture is, especially within the context of multicultural therapy. This is explored at some length by McLeod (1998) and other writers focusing on multicultural therapy (see for instance Lago and Thompson, 1996; Ponterotto et al., 1995; Sue and Sue, 1990).

Culture is a complex phenomenon and consequently it is important that therapists are cautious about the extent to which they can claim to understand any client's culture and its impact on them. Various writers have focused on the cultural beliefs underlying the various schools of therapy. Laungani (1997) points to the cultural incongruence that often occurs between client and therapist in client-centred therapy. Lago and Thompson (1996) review the three waves of therapy and produce the following list of cultural beliefs emanating from them:

1   The theories are based on the idea of 'the individual', defined as a belief that individuals are in charge of their own destiny.
2   Humans are in a constant state of flux, of movement, of 'becoming'.
3   There is a requirement to be active in one's life, not passive.
4   The process of growth through therapy is to throw off or shed the effects of parental, family and community influences that have had perceived negative effects.
5   The challenge is to live authentically in the social world, to be truly oneself.
6   As human beings we have scientific/rational tendencies.
7   The world is as we perceive it to be.
8   The sanctity of personal authority is not questioned, which implies that:
9   All parental and cultural values are open to questioning, and
10 The concept of personal choice is highly valued.

Patterson (1996) argues strongly against applying culturally specific techniques to ethnic minority groups. He points out that:

1   Descriptions of such groups are generalizations and can lead to cultural stereotypes.
2   Self-fulfilling prophecy can result if we treat people as if they fit such stereotypes, for example blanket statements that non-Western clients need a more structured approach, need more direction and guidance from their counsellor.
3   Knowledge of the client's culture may not of itself lead to better therapy.
4   Directive, guiding, active therapy, which is often recommended for clients from ethnic minority group, has not been shown to be effective or competent.
5   Self-disclosure by the client is a necessary part of successful therapy, however difficult, however Western.
6   There is a danger of abandoning or watering down what we know to be effective therapy.

Patterson tellingly comments that research does not as yet back the use of culturally specific techniques. However, this could reflect the overall relative lack of research into therapy and the limitations of existing studies.

Patterson's (1996) view was immediately challenged by McFadden (1996) and Pedersen (1996). McFadden (1996) maintains that a multicultural approach does not mean the abandonment of traditional counselling or its dilution. He regards the traditional theory base of counselling and psychotherapy as derived from work with the socially, financially and educationally privileged. Pedersen (1996) argues that it is a false dichotomy to suggest that a multicultural counsellor either be universal or allow each particular cultural group to define its own rules. He invites us to recognize counselling's antecedents in our own and other people's cultures so that we can realize how time and culturally specific many current practices in counselling are. He insists that 'multicultural skills means having the ability to use time-bound and cultural-bound theories, tests, or techniques in culturally appropriate ways' (1996: 236).

I think the argument that we all inhabit a variety of cultures and subcultures is valid, and we as therapists need to listen to and learn what cultures our clients belong to and what they mean for them in particular. Nevertheless it is also crucial and respectful to be aware of the main cultural currents that our clients come from, especially those from minority cultures including religious and spiritual minorities, be this Islam, Buddhism, Sikh, Hindu, Judaism, New Age, new religious, or whatever. It can be too easy to make assumptions about what being a Christian means also.

McLeod (1998) suggests that there are a number of underlying cultural aspects that therapists working within the West are likely to embody without necessarily being aware of them. These include:

1　The concept of reality – whether it is the still dominant mind/body duality of the West or the more traditional holistic view to be found in Buddhism, Hinduism and other Eastern belief systems.
2　The sense of self, autonomous or collectivist: how morality is constructed, whether it is seen as individual choice and responsibility or as fate or karma.
3　Whether the focus on time is future orientated or related back to family and ancestors.
4　How many in the West live miles away from their place of birth in contrast to more traditional societies.

This then is the background to multicultural therapy. It has profound implications for the client's and therapist's spirituality, which receives all too little discussion in the literature. Typically religion is mentioned in passing in phrases which talk about 'respect for client's religious beliefs'. Or religion and spirituality are discussed in the context of traditional healers or shamans (see Chapter 1 for a discussion of shamans).

Many people belonging to ethnic minority groups in the West do still consult traditional healers who are often religious or spiritual leaders in their community, and therapists are advised to work in co-operation with them (Lee- and Armstrong, 1995). Indeed, we find that 'within many cultural groups, there is often little distinction made between spiritual existence and secular life' (1995: 451). For such groups the healing or therapeutic help offered will intrinsically be seen as spiritual. However, Lee and Armstrong comment: 'Many Western helpers are trained to offer their services in a manner that generally ignores or discounts these notions of spirituality' (1995: 448).

Gergen, whose ideas are further explored in the next chapter, suggests that in our postmodern world therapy is especially valuable in dealing with the inner chaos that can arise when families and communities fragment:

> And with the disappearance of communities, with the disappearance of others who are stable, the therapeutic community has everything to gain. It is a requirement of postmodern culture. We stand in for lost communities, lost friends, lost intimates and that I think is highly understandable to the culture. (1996: 6)

I find this notion that somehow therapy can 'stand in' for the loss of community and intimate friends very disturbing. However, I think Gergen is making a vitally important point about the collapse of communities in urban Western societies.

It is therefore highly likely for the multicultural therapist to be working with clients who are experiencing cultural tensions. An example from my own work involved a female client of Asian background, born and brought up in Britain and now at university. She was under pressure from her parents to give up her studies and agree to an arranged marriage. If she refused this pressure she was in conflict with her family's culture; if she accepted it she went against the Western culture of her university and of her own desire to marry someone she chose and loved. There is no easy answer to such a cross-cultural dilemma. Either choice will result in considerable pain for the client.

It is too easy for Western therapists to take a Western view of such a client's dilemma and maintain that she should marry whom she chooses. It is of crucial importance to explore what her choices mean to her, including the part her family's culture plays in her life.

In this context the choice by this client of seeing a secular Western therapist is of interest. She could for example have sought help from within her family's cultural tradition, perhaps from a religious leader. She chose instead to go outside her culture. The question that then arises is: is the therapist she consults equipped to be sufficiently understanding of a culture where arranged marriages are the norm?

In the mid 1980s a client who was a Sikh came to me for counselling. He was wrestling with how to pursue his faith in England: he had taken to wearing a turban and traditional clothes and had then abandoned them for Western clothes and hairstyle, but still wondered whether he had made the right decision. He had also separated from his wife and this was causing him some upset and concern. I was struck at the time by two things. Firstly, it was not clear that he could be happy with either choice, being Western or being a Sikh. Secondly, he wanted me to be a man of standing in the local community, something of a wise man leading a settled married life, perhaps akin to a spiritual teacher or elder of the community who could offer sound advice. Of course I did not offer him advice and guidance and I was neither really a wise man nor settled at that time. This could and was explored in terms of transference on his part but it also represents something of a different model, from out of his culture, of what he needed in a counsellor.

In the late 1980s and early 1990s I made three work trips to Japan which each lasted a fortnight. I ran therapy groups and gave individual sessions, all with the aid of an interpreter (to my shame!), although many of the people I worked with spoke and understood American English. After a few days on each trip I found that I was intensely lonely in a way that was new to me and I called it 'cultural loneliness'. I found myself longing for simple English conversations about the weather or the state of the railways. This was despite the fact that one of my two hosts was American.

On the therapeutic groups I facilitated I found that the cultural barriers would go down and that the Japanese people on the groups, although perhaps not typical Japanese people, would speak of relationship difficulties, problems with their families of origin, and work issues, with much of the same pain, anger and suffering as I had seen expressed in similar groups in Britain, Switzerland and Ireland. However, occasionally I had a strange feeling that the whole group of Japanese people was somehow alien to me, or was a different species from me. There was no sense of superiority or inferiority in this feeling, just difference. Then the moment would pass. I still remember the joy I felt when I returned to England and overheard ordinary conversations on the London Underground about the weather and London traffic.

Although this challenge of living and working in a multicultural society has been insufficiently addressed by many therapists and therapist training courses, at least it does receive some consideration. Some of the crudest elements of racism and sexism have been and continue to be challenged. There is of course much more work to be done including deeply questioning whether the white Western middle class structure and values of counselling and psychotherapy provide an appropriate and effective form of help to people from other cultures. Addressing such questions might well have the added benefit of raising the issue of whether therapy is such a panacea for Western culture. Perhaps we have a lot to learn from other ways of living and caring for one another.

What is harder for Western therapists and their trainers to address is the role of religion in the life of many people from other cultures. At times I sense almost an embarrassment on the part of the white therapist when faced with clear statements of, say, Islamic faith which of course challenges the popular media image of Islamic fundamentalism. If the health of such faith is acknowledged the therapist will possibly be challenged to review her or his own religious upbringing.

How can we value and acknowledge our clients' religious faiths if we do not value and recognize our own, or our own questioning and awareness of issues like death and loss? Even if we truly are atheists and have resolved any religious tensions and dilemmas we might have, can we sit comfortably with our clients' expressions of faith without regarding them as something less, somehow inferior to us? Can we truly be accepting of their difference to us? Can we admit the possibility that religion is healthy to them? Can we accept the New Age exploration of many young people in our society without dismissing it as do-it-yourself religion (as if Christianity was not similarly created at some stage!)? I feel it is impossible to be indifferent to this issue. Sometimes it will not matter at all, other times it will be crucial, and our clients will challenge us to be honest about how we feel about their beliefs. We at least owe them the respect of having examined ourselves deeply on these issues prior to the therapeutic encounter.

In developing our understanding of the various cultures and subcultures now present and part of British life it is important not to make assumptions about the religious or spiritual beliefs of a particular client based merely on their ethnic background. It is necessary to include spiritual questions in the assessment of clients for therapy (discussed in Chapter 6) or in some other way find out the significance or otherwise of spirituality for the client.

RELIGIOUS THERAPIES?

There are a number of therapeutic approaches that are explicitly religious, namely ones which draw explicitly on the concepts and practices of a particular religion. Growing in size and popularity in Britain are the various branches of Buddhism, which have in particular made inroads among therapists, a number of whom are now using psychotherapeutic techniques drawn from Buddhism (e.g. Brazier, 1996; Donington, 1994; Sills, 1996; de Silva, 1993; 1996). 'Counselling needs to draw upon a wide range of sources, and Buddhism happens to be one among these sources and a particularly rich one at that' (de Silva, 1993: 33).

David Brazier advocates a Zen Buddhist approach to therapy and provides us with a succinct description of its key characteristics which conveys something of its appeal:

Some of the primary characteristics of Zen therapy which distinguishes it from most western therapies are its grounding in Buddhist psychology and karmic causality: not placing the 'self' at the centre of the universe; its valuing of the therapeutic power of aesthetics and of contact with nature; the importance it attaches to aloneness, silence and stillness; its advancement of mindfulness and awareness as the way to transcend the expression–repression dichotomy; its willingness to use responses which jolt the client's established assumptions and habits; its acceptance that shame has a therapeutic value; the importance it attaches to role reversal and service to others; its emphasis on simplicity and non-accumulation; and last, but by no means least, its totally different assessment of the role of childhood experience in the development of personality and its non-blaming attitude towards parents. (1996: 16)

De Silva (1993) points us to the long tradition of Buddhist monks providing counselling for the wider community. De Silva not only suggests the value of using Buddhist techniques in therapy with those of a Buddhist faith where the usual Western approaches may have limited appeal and success, but suggests they have a wider usage. For instance, Buddhist literature contains references to a large number of specific strategies for behavioural change that are similar to and predate many modern cognitive and behavioural techniques:

The repertoire of specific techniques that Buddhism has for counselling is impressive indeed. These include: systematic use of rewards and punishment; fear reduction by graded exposure; modelling; self-monitoring; stimulus control; overt and covert aversion; use of family members for implementing a behaviour-change programme; and specific techniques, including distraction and over-exposure, for unwanted intrusive cognitions. (1993: 32)

A clear case is thus made by de Silva for the incorporation of techniques drawn from Buddhism into the practice of counselling and psychotherapy.

Parry and Jones (1996) develop further the value of a Buddhist perspective for practising therapists when they maintain that belief in the reality of a separate self actually adds to human suffering, and consequently: 'It follows that therapies that themselves accept uncritically the notion of the Self are clinging to the suffering they aim to alleviate' (1996: 177).

While Brazier offers us Zen therapy and De Silva offers us the chance to draw on Buddhist techniques, core process therapy developed by Maura Sills:

incorporates a wide range of concepts and skills that have been developed in the West, but the conceptual framework, the focus on awareness and presence in the work, derives from a Buddhist perspective, though the work itself requires no special commitment to Buddhism. (Donington, 1994: 51)

The list provided by De Silva is very much at a technique level, in contrast to Brazier's paper which focuses almost exclusively on the theoretical level, whilst the core process approach seems to offer more of a true marriage between Western therapy and Buddhism. However, it is one thing to make appropriate use of techniques drawn integratively or eclectically from a range of sources; it is another matter to attempt to integrate on a theoretical level. One is left asking a similar question one asks of Christian counsellors: are they counsellors who happen to be Christian, or Christians who happen to counsel? In other words, which is the bigger picture – psychology or spirituality/religion? One answer offered by Benner (1988) is to suggest that the spiritual and the psychological are not to be neatly separated, and he talks of a 'psychospiritual unity'. This phrase has been taken up by the PsychoSpiritual Initiative (discussed in Chapter 5) and there is a grouping of therapists who call themselves 'psychospiritual' therapists in contrast to the label 'transpersonal' therapists, which is explored by Jones (1996) and others (Brazier, 1996; Sills, 1996; Whitmore, 1996) in a recent edition of *Self & Society*.

However, I am left with a further thought: what about the phrase 'spiritopsyche', which would indicate that the spiritual is the first and last consideration rather than the psychological? Perhaps that takes us well beyond therapy and towards the realm of spiritual direction and guidance which will be further explored in Chapter 9.

Finally, like all religions Buddhism is a human creation, if metaphysically inspired, and some of its followers are inevitably less than perfect. In Chapter 7 I discuss a client (see Case 2) who suffered a great deal whilst living in a Buddhist community.

Having explored the role Buddhism has played within psychotherapy, it is at least worth touching on the part played by Christianity. As we saw in Chapter 1, therapy has its origins in Christian and non-Christian practices of caring for the sick and providing soul care, and many counselling agencies have Christian founders. Probably the largest such agency world-wide is Alcoholics Anonymous (AA). AA was founded by two alcoholics who were Christians, but as an organization AA aims to be spiritual rather than religious or denominational in its approach. Its 12-step approach to alcoholism has been used with other addictions including drugs, work, overeating and sex. The strength of such an approach lies in the great capacity for mutual support, offered by others facing the same difficulties. The starting point or first step is that of the person admitting their inability or helplessness in dealing with their problem and that a greater (spiritual) power is available to help them:

> The 12-step programs view spirituality in recovery from addiction as the basis of a lifestyle change. Rather than deny the reality of his or her condition, the addict must begin to see the addiction as destructive to the self . . . Acknowledgement of one's helplessness leads to the recognition that one must turn to something outside of the self to begin the process of recovery . . . That something outside of the self that will support recovery is the higher power. (Hopson, 1996: 536–7)

There is also an understanding that the quest that compelled the person towards the addiction can be redirected towards the higher power, that is that the addiction can be seen as a degenerate form of spiritual development. The 12-step programmes are non-denominational although some groups do use the Bible or other spiritual texts. Secular versions of the 12-step programme have also been developed.

Although the 12-step programme is based on self-help, or 'altruism' in the words of AA, it is quite common for individuals in a programme to also seek help from professional therapists. I describe in Chapter 7 my experience of working with one such client. I was impressed by how much support was available to my client via her fellow ex-addicts in AA, and how such support seemed to aid, complement and speed up the progress of her therapy. It also felt as if the AA programme stood in place of a Church or religious group for her.

There are a number of mainstream therapists who are open about their Christian spirituality and religious beliefs. One of these is Brian Thorne, a person-centred counsellor and professor, who writes:

> As a Christian therapist I believe that I am accompanied always by my Lord and I know assuredly that it is the operation of grace which heals and brings wholeness . . . I am convinced that where love, acceptance, cherishing, understanding and compassion are present, then God is in the midst and grace is available. (1988: 213)

When discussing his concept of 'tenderness' mentioned earlier, which occurred when he chose to trust the feeling of interrelatedness with a client, Thorne found that 'my client and I are caught up in a stream of love' as the first step towards 'a willingness on my part to acknowledge my spiritual experience of reality' (1991: 77).

Clearly Thorne is describing the mystical realm. However he has been heavily criticized for his case presentation of a client called Sally in which, spiritually motivated, he engaged in a naked embrace with her (Thorne, 1991). Inevitably questions do arise which are further touched on in Chapter 5, but does this invalidate Thorne's deep grasp of the relationship between therapy and spirituality? What is clear is that there are boundary issues to be considered when our work with clients becomes more overtly spiritual and more overtly interconnected, which will be discussed further in Chapter 8.

Thorne (1994) also puts forward a five-point programme of what he calls 'developing a spiritual discipline' for the would-be effective person-centred therapist. The points are: focusing on his relationship with his body; focusing on his relationship with others (excluding clients); focusing on his use of time; awareness of the created order around him; and finally putting himself in the presence of God.

In addition to these practices for maintaining himself as an effective therapist he also holds in his mind his absent client each day:

> The discipline is simple: it consists of focusing on each client in turn, bringing him or her to mind and calling up a visual image of the person in question. The counsellor then holds the client in a metaphysical embrace of acceptance and understanding for a minute or two. (1994: 47)

The clients involved do not necessarily know about this spiritual practice conducted on their behalf by Brian Thorne. Interestingly, my research into Quaker therapists (West, 1998a) found that almost three-quarters of the sample of 18 prayed for their clients, sometimes inside sessions, and two of them described on occasions 'holding their clients in the light' which is akin to what Thorne describes previously.

No discussion of religious therapy would be complete without a mention of Frank Lake, psychiatrist, evangelical Christian and originator of clinical theology. Clinical theology was influenced by primal therapy and Lake (1981) increasingly saw people's troubles as stemming from traumatic pre-birth experiences that could be worked with therapeutically. He related human suffering explicitly to Christ's suffering and was known to pray with his clients at the start of a therapy session.

In Chapter 4 in the section entitled 'New Age Spirituality' I also explore how some humanistic therapists' work is influenced by their New Age beliefs.

THE FAITH OF THE THERAPISTS

Psychologists who affirmed Christian beliefs tended to endorse the cognitive-behavioral orientation, and those who affirmed Eastern and mystical beliefs tended to endorse humanistic and existential orientations. (Bilgrave and Deluty, 1998: 329)

Halmos (1965) insisted that counselling is a faith activity based on love rather than a neutral scientific procedure. In the USA several surveys have explored the religious beliefs of therapists (Bergin, 1980; Bergin and Jensen, 1990; Shafranske and Malony, 1985; 1990). The therapists surveyed showed low rates of conventional religious affiliation and participation in contrast to their clients. However Bergin and Jensen (1990) discovered 'a substantial amount of religious participation and spiritual involvement among all groups of therapists beyond or in addition to traditional conventions'.

This finding was supported by the Shafranske and Malony study in which over half of their psychologist respondents regarded their spirituality as an 'alternative spiritual path which is not part of organized religion' (1990: 74).

In my own research into therapists whose work includes healing (West, 1997) I found that the majority of my respondents, admittedly a small qualitative sample of 30, met their spiritual and religious needs through unorthodox spiritual or healing groups rather than through conventional religion. As one respondent put it, 'I am not religious but I'm quite spiritual.' It is possible to regard practising as a therapist as a spiritual activity or process, which I have explored in some detail elsewhere (West, 1998b).

Bilgrave and Deluty (1998) in their survey of 237 US clinical and counselling psychologists found that 66 per cent of them believed in the transcendent, 72 per cent believed that their religious beliefs affected their clinical practice of therapy, and 66 per cent believed that their practice of therapy affected their religious beliefs. Those who affirmed Eastern and mystical beliefs tended to be humanistic or existential in orientation, while curiously those who affirmed Christianity were more likely to be cognitive-behavioural in approach. The authors suggest that orthodox Christianity conflicts with core humanistic and psychodynamic views. Atheists and agnostics were more likely to be psychodynamic, as were Jews. They conclude:

> This study found that many psychologists possess personal *Weltanschauungen* that include distinctly religious beliefs, consider these beliefs personally important, use these beliefs to help guide their practice of psychotherapy, and, conversely, use their practice of psychotherapy to modify these beliefs. (1998: 346)

This whole question of the faith of the therapist can be applied to the founders of modern psychotherapy and counselling. Suzanne Kirschner (1996) argues that contemporary Anglo-American psychoanalytic theory presents models that use the same narrative pattern as that of older spiritual and cultural structures and themes. In particular she mentions the Christian doctrine of fall and redemption which was secularized during the early nineteenth century by Romantic philosophers before being taken up into psychoanalytic theory.

Other writers have commented on the cultural and religious origins of Freud, Jung and Rogers (see Feltham, 1995; Fuller, 1984; McLeod, 1993; 1998; Sollod, 1978) and how the therapeutic approaches they developed owe a lot to this. Sollod (1978) draws our attention to Rogers's strong Protestant background: he was born into a strict ascetic and religious family and had a desire early on in his life to become a minister. Sollod also points out what he regards as the features of client-centred therapy that are Protestant in style. These include: the focus on the individual working out their own destiny without interference; the trust in feelings and intuition to guide the process; the emphasis on the here-and-now; and the non-authoritarian relationship between therapist and client that is analogous to that of the clergy and laity in the Protestant Church.

According to Fuller there is a tradition within American spirituality that maintains that individuals 'have an innate psychological capacity to apprehend – and become inwardly connected to an immanent divinity' (1984: 31). Fuller reckons that Rogers translated such religious beliefs into secular and psychological terms and that his therapeutic theories arose from his early religious upbringing.

Sollod contrasts this Protestant flavour of client-centred therapy with the almost rabbinic quality of psychoanalysis: 'here the trust is in the trained reason of the therapist (rabbi) and in his Talmudic interpretations of complex phenomena' (1978: 96). The focus is now on the effect of the client's past on their present life and the use of reason to help the client's self-understanding. Freud was not brought up as a practising Jew but throughout his life he wrestled with what religion meant to people, returning time and time again to consider it (discussed in Hay, 1982; Symington, 1994). However, this view of Freud's debt to his religious origins is challenged by Vitz (1993) who argues that Freud was in fact more influenced by Christian literature and theology than by Judaism.

Jung's father was a minister who lost his faith but continued his work as the local priest (Jung, 1967). Jung himself was not conventionally religious but he came to value the spiritual part played by authentic religion as discussed above. Gerard Egan (1990), the developer of the 'skilled helper' eclectic style of counselling, trained and practised as a Catholic priest before embarking on an academic career. He is based at Loyala University in Chicago and his writings clearly show signs of his Jesuit upbringing. His systematic approach to self-awareness has echoes of the spiritual exercises of St Ignatius. Despite this his writings rarely mention religion or spirituality and his whole approach is accessible to the most secular of practitioners.

This brief survey illustrates how modern psychotherapy, having developed within Judaeo-Christian culture, is then shot through with elements of its spirituality reflected in its therapy and in the lives of many of its key founders. As Rogers (1980) himself stated towards the end of his life:

> Our experiences in therapy and in groups, it is clear, involve the transcendent, the indescribable, the spiritual. I am compelled to believe that I, like many others, have under-estimated the importance of this mystical, spiritual dimension.

However from our consideration of the main threads of therapy, it is clear that there remains much denial of the part played by spirituality in our culture and consequently in the growth and development of psychotherapy.

3

Some Issues in Therapy Today

In this chapter I will explore some issues relating to the current situation of therapy within Britain with regard to spirituality, focusing on the limits of secular therapy, the 'empty' or 'saturated' self of the individual in our modern consumer society, and the opportunity for spirituality to regain its part in the healing of people's woes. Finally I will explore the notion of counselling and psychotherapy as spiritual practices.

THE LIMITS OF (SECULAR) THERAPY

Counselling has increasingly become a source of public controversy. On the one hand there is almost a knee-jerk reaction to disasters of 'sending in the counsellors'. On the other hand there is much criticism in the press of counselling – of its apparent overuse, of whether it is effective, ethical or even desirable. It feels as if counselling has become the focus of public interest and concern in much the same way that social work was a decade or two ago. There is also more informed, more counsellor-friendly criticism advanced by people like Smail (1987) and Howard (1995) who challenge the therapy world to moderate its claims and more importantly to work with, rather than undermine, other, often informal, community based forms of caring.

Counselling is thus being tested in informed and ill-informed ways. It is estimated that over 50 per cent of GP surgeries now offer counselling and there are many statutory and voluntary agencies offering specialist forms of counselling. Gradually a picture is emerging of short-term, time-limited counselling as the most common form being offered, because of cost if nothing else, with a focus on a problem managing if not solving approach that can be flexible to the needs of the client.

Within this picture there is a shrinking, perhaps a realistic shrinking, of what counselling is seen to be able to achieve, with a lowering of hopes and a sense of the limitations, a focus on small and measurable outcomes. In this context Gerard Egan's (1990) model of problem management as a form of helping has become popular on counsellor training courses. Such a model reduces the radical nature of using Rogers's (1951) core conditions of empathy, congruence and unconditional positive regard to merely being a way of developing an effective therapeutic alliance. Within this alliance an agenda for change, or at least problem management, is set by the client with the counsellor's help.

Such an approach can present a real challenge to the faith of the counsellors. The language used switches away from growth and even cure towards problem management. This may well reflect a realistic response to very difficult problems faced by clients and the limited resources offered by way of counselling. Also it is perhaps a response to the limits of any one counsellor and their ability to be an agent of support and hopefully change for the client.

There is, however, a sense of loss in this lowering of expectations and perhaps even the client suffers from the therapist's lowered expectation. Maybe the clients live down to these lowered expectations. In contrast the spiritually minded therapist is always open to the possibility of God's grace in Christian terms or its equivalent in other faiths. This implies that somehow more possibilities for growth and change will be available than indicated by the usual skills of the therapist. Over three-quarters of the Quaker therapists I interviewed (West, 1998a) said that their spiritual faith gave them something extra when they worked. As one put it:

> What supports me is really the silence, and the belief, and sometimes the awareness of an unseen third party in the form of spirit, which is perhaps the most vital and healing agent. It is a three-way process: there are two people, their two souls and the Other in the room.

However, such potential for 'something extra' being available is not exclusive to the religiously minded therapist (Clarkson, 1990). The therapeutic encounter can take on the quality of Buber's (1970) I–Thou relationship. A possibility exists that neither client nor therapist needs to be limited by their own shortcomings and failings. The possibility is that *metanoia*, a real change of heart, can occur in the client (and in the therapist too), that there are no limits to the changes that can happen when the time and situation are ripe. Have secular counsellors given up their faith in the healing power of love for minimal progress through the management of problems? Is this the vision and legacy of the Thatcher and Reagan era?

THE EMPTY SELF, THE SATURATED SELF AND POSSIBLE SELVES

In a key article in the *American Psychologist* in 1990 Philip Cushman argued, albeit from within the US tradition, that the self can now be contextualized as 'empty' in contrast to the earlier sexually restricted self of the Victorian era. Cushman says of this empty self: 'by this I mean that our terrain has shaped a self that experiences a significant absence of community, tradition, and shared meaning' (1990: 600). This empty self has then to be filled up with food, consumer products and the lives of media celebrities. 'It is a self that seeks the experience of being continually filled

up by consuming goods, calories, experiences, politicians, romantic part-
ners, and empathic therapists in an attempt to combat the growing
alienation and fragmentation of its era' (1990: 600).

Cushman argues that the two professions most responsible for healing or
at least filling this empty self are advertising and psychotherapy. He further
suggests that since psychotherapy cannot and will not address the historic
causes of the empty self it ends up like advertising in proposing a lifestyle
solution which brings with it a greater possibility of abuse occurring
within the therapeutic relationship.

Psychotherapy individualizes a problem that has arisen for the client
within a cultural context which is not usually adequately addressed during
therapy, and results in therapy perpetuating the problem. Putting it in a
historic context:

> Americans in the post-World War II era came to need self-improvement in a
> form and to a degree unknown before . . . The cosmetics industry, the diet
> business, the electronic entertainment industry, preventive medical care, and
> the self-improvement industry (containing mainstream psychology, pop psy-
> chology, and pop religion) all came to prominence. (Cushman, 1990: 603–4)

With an empty self people are always in need. This inner emptiness is
expressed according to Cushman via low self-esteem, values confusion,
eating disorders, drug abuse, chronic consumerism and a hunger for spiritual
guidance. In this gap left by the decline of tradition, families, communities
and culture we find that psychotherapy is less of a scientific cure and more a
'covert vehicle for cultural guidance and transmission' (1990: 606).

Although psychotherapy claims to systematically uncover, resolve and
work through the causes of the individual's ills, Cushman suggests that:

> without the therapist being aware of it, practice deviates from normative
> discourse by allowing the therapist to function as a model for the patient, by
> providing corrective emotional experiences of care, respect, and understanding,
> and by allowing the patient to 'take in' the therapist's ideas, values, and
> personal style. (1990: 606)

This matches my own observation that successful clients often learn how
to be clients, that we therapists, in effect, teach our clients a form of
choreography: they dance to our tunes, they dream in our frameworks,
they borrow our words using the appropriate psychospeak, be it psychodynamic, person-centred or eclectic. They learn to be like us. The more
they succeed in this task, the more they appear 'cured'. Notice how some
psychotherapists will not work with clients who 'cannot establish a suitable
therapeutic relationship' or who are not 'psychologically minded'. This
begs so many questions. Notice also how many of our successful clients go
on indeed to be more like us and train as therapists or counsellors. As a
trainer of counsellors I sometimes wonder if I am not involved in some
form of pyramid selling in which experienced counsellors go on to
become trainers, supervisors and therapists to other counsellors.

Cushman suggests that the most important function currently of psychotherapy is that it offers an alternative attitude towards life, cultural values and practices. In conclusion he argues that therapy's individualizing of society's problems is a poor form of treatment:

> The central point of my argument is that in a world sorely lacking in community and tradition, the most effective healing response would be to address those absences through structural societal change by reshaping political relationships and cultural forms and reestablishing the importance of their transmission. (1990: 607)

Although Cushman's arguments could be dismissed as applying only to the USA, his words do seem applicable to the current situation in postmodern Britain today. Other writers within Britain have addressed the issue of why we seem to need so much counselling and psychotherapy and how appropriate this is. (See for instance Dryden and Feltham, 1992; Howard, 1995; Smail, 1987.) Cushman, however, advances a clear and historically based argument for the current ills of the West.

Besides Cushman's view of the self as empty we have the 'saturated self' of Kenneth Gergen (1991; 1996). Gergen suggests that in advanced capitalist economies we can now have global relationships reflected in the various roles we are free to take via the Internet, television, faxes, mobile phones and travel. We can become different selves in different situations. This can result in fragmentation, multiple personalities or subselves. We can then have a choice of a number of possible selves and this has problematic consequences.

Gergen (1996) suggests that one of the implications of the 'saturated self' of modern advanced capitalist societies is an increasing recognition of how reality is a construct, how it has become increasingly hard to hold onto one's cultural's view of, and construction of, reality. Gergen (1996) feels like Cushman that we have a sense of the emptying of the self and a loss of community which can lead to an increased valuing of relationship and a sense of interconnectedness which may even be experienced as global.

THE OPPORTUNITY FOR SPIRITUALITY

Therapists are of course not immune to these wider changes in society, reflected in the breakdown of family and community life in Britain – changes which are only partially paralleled by the growth of new forms of living. We have noted earlier how the decline in the clergy in both Britain (Halmos, 1965) and the USA (Nelson and Torrey, 1973) has been matched by the increase in the number of counsellors. The implication was that people are now taking problems to therapists that they might have previously taken to clergy or other workers in the Church. Of course the

Church has in many places got on the counselling bandwagon. However, here it has often faced a dilemma: whether to stay within the largely secular counselling approach or hang onto the often rather rigid articles of faith. Neither answer has proved totally satisfactory. For if your priest or rabbi counsels you without any spiritual content, why not choose a secular therapist instead? Likewise if your priest comes over as very religiously dogmatic, you may again wish you had chosen a secular counsellor. There are definite role conflicts and boundaries here. Of course I am presenting a rather polarized position but nevertheless it holds some truth (for a discussion of this and other related issues see Lyall, 1995). Rowan (1993), as mentioned earlier in a criticism of Jung, suggested that not everything spiritual can and should be psychologized. However, we do need an awareness of how there can be a flight into religion as a defence against our problems.

As a trainer of counsellors I am amazed at the number of people who come forward for counsellor training even though there are very few full-time jobs being created for counsellors, and the occasional part-time post can attract hundreds of applications. It seems at times as if the counselling world itself constitutes a religion or at least a faith. Halmos (1965) insisted that the faith of the counsellors was in the power of love. This could take us close to a spiritual position if we consider the Christian concept of agape, or God as love (Peck, 1990), or the Buddhist emphasis on compassion.

What is striking is that despite the decline in conventional religion there is a huge increase in retreat-going (Hughes, 1989) and spiritual direction and friendship (Leech, 1994), often by people lacking a strong connection with religion (further discussed in Chapter 9). There is also an increase in courses of various kinds offering some element of the spiritual approach to life.

COUNSELLING AND PSYCHOTHERAPY AS SPIRITUAL PRACTICES

Counselling and psychotherapy are not the same as spirituality and religion. It is a mistake to psychologize religion and to maintain that religion has the answer to all problems addressed by psychotherapy. Our therapy clients do need more than the right passage from the Bible or the Koran, adjustment to their Buddhist meditation practices, or a spiritual sermon. Indeed, one of the insights offered by Ken Wilber and discussed in Chapter 6, is the notion that some aspects, some problems of human development are best helped via therapy in some instances and spiritual guidance in others. Wilber presents a much debated model that offers us insight into which is best with which problem by a process of locating at what stage the client is in terms of their development.

Spirituality and therapy do offer differing ways of addressing the ills of mankind and have differing views of healthy human development. However, the differences between say transpersonal psychotherapy and cognitive behaviourism is as large as that between Buddhism and fundamentalist Christianity.

What I find of interest is to view counselling and psychotherapy as spiritual practices. This can be taken in three different ways: that the therapists can regard their work as a spiritual practice; that the client can regard their therapy as spiritual; and that some or all of what happens within the therapy room is seen by either or both as a spiritual process. Let us consider each in turn.

In my research into Quakers who were therapists (West, 1998a) I found not surprisingly that nearly three-quarters of those I interviewed agreed with the statement that 'My spiritual faith underpins all of my therapy work.' Indeed for some it seemed to go further than just underpinning: 'I couldn't divorce my own faith and spiritual experience, such as it is, from the work I do'; and 'I am what I am and I bring that to whatever I do, including counselling.'

The question that then immediately arises is: does this make a difference and do their clients know? My research showed that almost three-quarters of the 18 therapists involved were at times inspired in a therapy session in a way similar to ministry in a Quaker meeting, the implication being that they are receiving spiritual inspiration during therapy sessions. Such inspirations can then be used, if appropriate, to benefit the client's therapy. For example, 'I can find myself making a suggestion about something or saying something to a client which I don't feel comes entirely from me.'

I discuss this use of spiritual inspiration further in Chapter 7. What is also apparent is that the clients involved will not necessarily realize that anything different or 'spiritual' is occurring, though one of my respondents was clear that such inspiration could occur equally to therapist or client.

It is also possible to view the whole practice of being a therapist as being spiritual. For instance the typical analytic and humanistic therapist remains very attentive to what their clients are saying, remains aware of their own responses to their clients, which can include awareness of their own body sensations and emotions. At the same time their attention remains focused on their client rather than on themselves. Such an approach is akin to, if not identical with, the spiritual practice of mindfulness:

> Eastern spiritual traditions have specific techniques for developing mindfulness, usually formal meditation practices of some sort . . . These Eastern practices consider the development of mindfulness as an ultimate goal, leading to enlightenment. (Tart and Deikman, 1991: 29)

Deikman (1982) regards the developing of an observing self as an important activity in both meditation and psychotherapy and as a link between them. However, he insists in his interview with Charles Tart (Tart and Deikman, 1991) that in meditation the person can still hide from themselves in a way that a psychotherapist would probably challenge.

Although both Eastern and Western approaches to growth value mindfulness, they 'have a different set of beliefs of what human beings ultimately are and what their possibilities are. In this sense, Western psychotherapy has a very limited view of what a person can be, compared to the mystical traditions (both Eastern and Western)' (1991: 39–40).

Deikman feels that the goal of psychotherapy and of spiritual development is the same, namely that of increased realism. He feels that people need to be ready for the spiritual path in a way not necessary for psychotherapy. Indeed he believes that Western psychotherapy 'can help set the stage for a much broader advance in spiritual development than has been possible in the past' (1991: 51).

Other writers have drawn our attention to the overlap between therapy and religious practices. Zen Buddhism, which emphasizes the direct here-and-now experience of reality, has clearly impacted on Gestalt and other humanistic therapies. The analyst Fromm (1986) points to the parallels between psychoanalysis and Zen, especially de-repression and enlightenment. Watts (1961) draws our attention to the Taoist influences he discerns in Rogers's client-centred therapy.

Inevitably the client's process may strike them as being a spiritual one, whether or not their therapist views it to be so. The question that then arises is: can the therapist be involved and open to the client's exploring of what they take to be a spiritual process? At the point when a client utters the word 'spiritual', or even worse the word 'religious', a number of therapists will inevitably shrink away from such work and begin to think in terms of a referral to a priest, vicar or other spiritual leader. For the therapist with the courage to support the client's exploration of what they consider to be a spiritual process there is much to be gained, and the implications for the therapist's own spirituality can be profound.

It is possible to argue that all of what happens in a therapeutic encounter, indeed in any human encounter, is spiritual. Indeed we can view the whole of human existence as spiritual. However (see discussion of spirituality in Chapter 1), the word 'spiritual' is often reserved for peak experiences, for special moments of connectedness, for a special quality of human relating and relatedness. In Chapter 5 I explore the issues of the therapeutic room as a spiritual space and of some of the special or spiritual experiences that can occur. Here I wish to underline the fact that many people, both therapists and clients, have experiences in which the therapeutic encounter takes on for them a clearly spiritual quality.

In summary it is possible to view the special moments in therapy – for therapist, client or both – as being spiritual, or to see the whole of the client's therapy as a spiritual process or spiritual journey.

4

Spirituality in Britain Today

> As a culture we are separated from the sacred, the numinous, the mysterious. In grasping for control and knowledge we have lost a sense of what is whole and holy. (Reason, 1994)

> Secularism – at least in any developed sense – remains the creed of a relatively small minority. (Davie, 1994: 69)

It is important when we are considering spirituality and therapy to be aware of the current situation of spirituality and religion in Britain today. This is a vast topic, a careful consideration of which could and does run to a number of books (see for instance Barker, 1989; Brierley, 1991; Bruce, 1995a; Davie, 1994; Walker, 1998). What I wish to do here is to paint some broad strokes that are especially relevant to this book and which will enable us to put therapeutic work with clients into a spiritual context.

The multicultural nature of British society is reflected in the post-war growth of Jewish, Muslim, Hindu, Buddhist, Sikh, New Age, pagan and other religious groups. Apart from the growth of institutions reflecting the more traditional non-Christian faiths there is also the emergence of non-Christian groups within the new religious movements discussed later.

DECLINE IN THE CHRISTIAN CHURCHES

> Most British social scientists, historians, and church leaders think that Britain is now not very religious and was once markedly more so. (Bruce, 1995b: 417)

> Believing without belonging. (Davie, 1994: 19)

It is very apparent that the mainstream Christian Churches in Britain are in decline, with shrinking congregations becoming increasingly elderly, whether they be Church of England, Catholic, Methodist or other. The Catholic Church lists all those baptized and the Church of England likewise has far more people on its electoral rolls than actually attend its services. Even given these inflations of the figures, overall Christian Church membership is estimated to have been 27 per cent of the adult population of Britain in 1850, declining to 14 per cent in 1990 (Bruce, 1995b). The current figures are likely to be even lower. The MARC Europe survey of Trinitarian English Churches (Brierley, 1991) found that in England in 1979 11 per cent of the population attended church, by 1989 the figure was 10 per cent, and the forecast is 9 per cent by the year 2000. This figure of 9 per cent includes a forecast of an increase in numbers attending charismatic and Pentecostal churches.

Grace Davie (1994), exploring the MARC survey figures, points out how there are now more Roman Catholic church attenders than Anglican (2,044,911 to 1,808,174). Nevertheless 26.7 million British people in 1995 still owed some allegiance to the Anglican Church. She comments: 'The description of the Church of England as the church from which the English choose to stay away still . . . catches the religious mood of a significant proportion of the population' (1994: 49). The main free Churches in England and Wales – the Methodists, Congregationalists, Baptists and Presbyterians – peaked before the First World War and then declined by over one-third up to 1970. This grouping continues to decline with the exception of the Baptists.

The sense of Britain being a 'Christian' society, reflected in many children attending Church of England schools, churches and church Sunday schools, is, with the possible exception of the schools, vanishing. For instance it is no longer possible to assume a general grasp of Bible stories, and belief in Christian articles of faith has similarly declined (Bruce, 1995b). Church weddings are in decline – from 70 per cent in 1900 to 53 per cent in 1990 – as are christenings, which in the Church of England numbered 65 per cent of live births in 1902, declining to 27 per cent in 1993.

The one part of the Christian Church that is growing is the fundamentalist or evangelical wing, reflected in the house church movement (discussed below) and other charismatic groups, and the rise of the black Christian Church. Their success seems to be based on two aspects: Bible based 'answers' to modern dilemmas of life; and a strong sense of community.

HOUSE CHURCHES

The 'house church movement', which has shown the most striking growth in the last two decades (Davie, 1994), is probably not an appropriate label, indeed the groups themselves do not like it. However: 'The phrase "house church movement" has become one of those convenient labels that we stick onto a variety of churches because they seem to be outside typical Christian experience' (Walker, 1998: 33). We find that this phrase covers a number of different organizations; that house churches have become full-blown churches in their own right with home groups attached; and finally that there are house church groups within Catholicism and the Church of England. However, we can generalize and say that most house churches are largely outside the main denominations, many are evangelical, and most are Pentecostal.

Walker (1998) regards the house church movement as the most significant Christian movement to emerge in the last 50 years in Great Britain. Although influenced by similar groups in the USA it is very much a British movement. It grew into some prominence in the early 1980s but had already suffered a major split in the mid 1970s and has grown less rapidly since the late 1980s. Walker (1998) suggests that the maximum number of what he calls 'hard core Restorationists' (his word for house church groups) was never more than 40,000 at its peak in 1984–5. Since then other charismatic groups have emerged.

The house church groups have more women than men but the leadership is almost invariably male. Ethnically the movement is mostly white although there have been some efforts to recruit ethnic minority members. It has tended to focus on young families, with fewer single or older people. Regrettably such groups take a traditional attitude to sexual minorities: 'If you are homosexual or lesbian, however, you will not be welcome unless you are prepared to become heterosexual (or, at least, not practise homosexuality). Kingdom people believe that you can be supernaturally "delivered" from sexual perversions' (1998: 201).

Walker tells us what to expect at a house church gathering:

> You will be able to dance and use your body in worship . . . you will find clapping, hands raised (and shaking), and extempore crying and praying . . . Worship in church and the house group will be Pentecostal worship. 'Signs and wonders' are normal . . . you will find expectations are high that God will heal the sick and deliver people from demons . . . Elders will determine whether your sin or problem is of demonic origin or some other source . . . elders will help you to exercise the gifts of tongues and prophecy. (1998: 203–4)

Inevitably there will be casualties from such practices. INFORM (Information Network Focus on Religious Movements, founded by Professor Barker of the LSE and funded by the Home Office) is an information service on religious cults. Barker told Andrew Walker in 1988 that house groups came second only to Scientologists in the number of enquiries that they received. Walker (1998) comments however that house church groups were by far bigger in size than other new religious groups.

Another phenomenon that is occurring is the widespread use of alpha groups within the Church of England and other Churches. These courses are aimed at giving people a grounding in Christian theology within a friendly small group context that often includes meals. Each group has an experienced teacher. The alpha teachings are biblically based and aim to answer people's basic religious and spiritual questions. Regrettably the alpha courses in their literature take a negative attitude to homosexual men and women.

Although Christians may feel that they are in a declining minority in our secularized society, the dominant culture does still reflect Judaeo-Christian values. For example, we currently have a church-attending Prime Minister, and bishops of the Anglican Church still sit in the House of Lords, and of course the monarch remains Head of the Church of England. Jews, Muslims, Hindus, Sikhs and Buddhists are not likewise represented, or so visible, or seen as part of ordinary life in modern Britain. Indeed, other traditional religions in Britain – Judaism, Islam, Hinduism, Buddhism and Sikhism – are facing a somewhat similar challenge of declining numbers, again with some increase in fundamentalism. However, as ethnic minorities their faith is often sustained and conversely sustains them in the face of racial and other prejudice.

The number of Muslims in Britain is hard to determine but it was estimated at 1.1 million in 1990, although a smaller figure would represent those religiously active. It is important to realize that being ethnically Asian does not make one a Muslim and vice versa. It is worth mentioning in passing that the Salman Rushdie controversy, which raised many questions of a religious and racist nature, pointed to a key issue in our survey of spirituality in Britain. Can our largely secular society be accepting of very religiously committed people who feel deeply offended by blasphemy? (And of course our blasphemy laws only apply to Christianity!) And how do we square this with a commitment to free speech?

Jews have declined from around 400,000 in Britain in the 1950s to around 330,000 today (Davie, 1994). This decline is accounted for by migration to Israel, assimilation, marrying out and the decreasing size of families. Nevertheless the Jewish community in Britain is the fifth largest in the world. According to Bruce (1995a) there are about 400,000 Hindus in Britain and about the same number of Sikhs. In a letter to *The Guardian* newspaper (26 November 1998) John Macintyre of the Pagan Federation claimed that there were over 100,000 pagans in Britain.

NEW AGE SPIRITUALITY

> Under the banner of New Age are to be found a range of beliefs, therapies and practices by which religious or 'depth' experiences are explored and honed, and what are perceived or experienced as manifestations of the supra-empirical world are invoked or manipulated. (Northcott, 1992: 3)

Since New Age Spirituality is not organized as a Church or Temple with a clear creed or set of beliefs, it is hard to tell how many people are covered by the label 'New Age'. Clearly its practices have touched the lives of many people including therapists and their clients. One of the keys to understanding New Age Spirituality is to recognize that it is rooted in people's own experience of their spirituality. There have always been folk beliefs existing alongside and outside official religion – something Towler called 'common religion' and about which he says: 'It survives only because of its continued ability to express the transcendent element in people's experience, and to bestow meaning on what would otherwise be perplexing' (quoted in Hay, 1982: 155). The content of this common religion will vary from time to time, and perhaps one way of viewing

New Age Spirituality is to see its roots and its appeal in common religion: indeed, Davie (1994) suggests that New Age Spirituality could be seen as a millennium version of common religion.

John Sandford, in his foreword to *New Age Spirituality* (1993), suggests that there is a lower or common form of New Age Spirituality involving crude forms of divination, various occult practices and mind-altering drugs. However, he insists there is also a higher form in which people are exploring new ways of thinking about themselves, the world and God: 'This is the true New Age, and its ranks include scientists, psychologists, and members of established religious faiths and traditions, including mainstream Christian denominations' (1993: vii). One starts to ask then, as one did with the house church movement, where does New Age Spirituality end and Christianity begin? What is the boundary?

New Age Spirituality gets a bad press from theologians – 'I confess there is much in the New Age movement that I personally find bizarre and unacceptable' (Lyall, 1995: 116) – and therapists alike: 'As I look over the shelves of the New Age section in the bookshop, the only thing I can find in common between the books and equipment on show is that they are suitable for gullible people. There is a complete mixture of the good, the bad and the ugly' (Rowan, 1993: 12).

However, there are dissenting voices:

> I see New Age Spirituality as the religion of the individual. This means that, for me, New Age Spirituality recognizes two main tenets: the first is that there is a high degree of individuality in any expression of this aspect of oneself and the second is that, coexistent and complementary with this, there is a general recognition of the universality of all things. (Young, 1988: 195)

Courtney Young, a humanistic psychotherapist based in the Findhorn community, who is quoted above, epitomizes the challenge offered by New Age Spirituality to conventional religions, and also indicates why it is attractive to many people within the therapy world. Young's viewpoint fits well with that of John Heron (1992; 1998) whose criticism of Wilber's model of spiritual development is explored in Chapter 6.

This focus on individuality and on the Higher Self within New Age Spirituality – 'My Spirituality is an expression of myself trying to live in closer contact with my Higher Self, which I define as that part of me which recognizes and connects with God' (Young, 1988: 196) – leads naturally enough to harsh criticism from Christianity, where there are teachings which suggest a focus on becoming like Christ, serving one's fellow humans, surrendering to God: 'not my will but thy will be done'.

One of the key criticisms of humanistic therapy, indeed of New Age Spirituality, is the focus on individuality, on the self, as being narcissistic (Olds, 1993; Spangler, 1993) which in the USA has led to pejorative comments about the so-called 'me generation'. However, from a somewhat surprising source, namely pastoral theology, comes a defence, if of a critical kind, of New Age Spirituality by Michael Northcott: 'The setting of the self in a cosmological context whereby new energies are tapped and explored can be dismissed as narcissism only if the profound metaphysical shift which much New Age philosophy involves is ignored or set to one side' (1992: 18). Northcott believes that pastoral counselling has colluded in the body–mind split and in the exclusion of spirit that has happened in modern medicine. He maintains that New Age Spirituality challenges this.

From a theological perspective Matthew Fox (1993), the Dominican monk who advocates creation-centred spirituality, takes a critical look at New Age Spirituality and concludes that it cannot carry the weight of the changes needed for the approaching new era. Fox is, however, aware of how people are 'wounded by the Church'. (Such woundings and their healing are a key part of many people's therapeutic journey and may well be one reason why therapy is so critical of religion and spirituality.) Nevertheless Fox is clear that mainstream Christianity has much to learn from New Age Spirituality. The application of such learnings, according to Fox, should include: ceasing left-brain-itis (i.e. intellectualizing); rediscovering our doctrines in the light of a creation spirituality tradition; renewing forms of worship; leading the way in renewal of education; making a commitment to deep ecumenism; and rediscovering the pre-modern era (Fox believes that the mystics and theologians of the twelfth and early thirteenth centuries have much to offer us today).

Again from a theological perspective the US Methodist minister Olds (1993) puts forward 12 key themes of New Age Spirituality. These are that it:

1 affirms self's awareness of self
2 affirms personal choice and responsibility
3 offers personal access to the divine
4 has an emphasis on synergy
5 values human potential
6 values feelings
7 values immediacy
8 uses the power of positive thinking
9 has a theology of ecology
10 welcomes innocence, a childlike wonder and trust
11 rescues value, meaning and goodness in humankind and nature
12 emphasizes balance and harmony.

Olds (1993) also produces a list of the limitations of New Age Spirituality which in many ways could be seen as a mirror image of the above list. So affirming self's awareness of self becomes narcissism, valuing of feeling becomes a negating of intellectual activity, and so on.

Northcott (1992) is aware of the challenge presented by New Age Spirituality to Christianity. He argues that many New Agers are ex-Christians who felt their spiritual needs were not being met within the Church. He also points out how over-accommodating Christianity has been to secular society, whilst in contrast New Age Spirituality seeks to bring or restore spirituality to the heart of modern life: 'New Age is a protest at the nineteenth century abandonment by religion of science, cosmology, economics, and health. It represents a rejection of the secular rationalist and materialist tenor of science, industry, consumerism and official Western religion' (1992: 11).

Northcott further maintains that New Age Spirituality and Christian pastoral theology share a concern for wholeness and spiritual identity and he believes that both have been heavily influenced by the work of Carl Rogers. Both regard death and dying as important areas of concern and Northcott regards the work of Elizabeth Kubler Ross as an 'important bridge between New Age and pastoral theology' (1992: 12).

Spangler (1993), a New Age author and critic, suggests that the New Age represents what Thomas Kuhn calls a paradigm shift, that is a change in how we view and understand the world. Spangler also points out that New Age people following Buddhism, shamanism and Celtic spirituality are actually following traditional religious paths rather than deserving to be viewed as New Age. However, many New Age people are picking up on such approaches but mixing them eclectically.

More importantly, Spangler (1993) regards many New Age practices such as channelling, the use of crystals, tarot cards and other forms of divination as not necessarily new, or necessarily spiritual. He insists that many of these practices are best understood as psychological and to him they represent the narcissism of contemporary USA. To Spangler the idea of a coming New Age is an ancient one to be found in every culture. Consequently he suggests that we view it as a prophetic idea which offers a critique of Western civilization, and which became part of the developing counterculture in the USA and elsewhere during the 1960s and 1970s.

Despite its critics New Age Spirituality continues to be very popular. It is also often linked to complementary medicine and hence to counselling, and its approach of working out your own way to salvation in the here-and-now makes it especially attractive to therapists and clients of a humanistic or transpersonal orientation. Indeed at times it appears as if the humanistic therapy world can be a substitute for religion, an idea explored by Sabine Kurjo who poses the question: 'Does it [humanistic psychology] not maybe have the potential to serve as the new religion, a new unifying force world-wide?' (1988: 229). Unfortunately having posed this intriguing question she does not fully answer it. However the fact that such a question is raised does show how far humanistic therapy overlaps with spirituality. This truth is reflected in the increasing popularity of courses which are part therapeutic, part New Age.

One clear point of connection between New Age Spirituality and humanistic and transpersonal therapy is the focus on experiencing. Kurjo draws attention to the value that humanistic therapy places on personal experiencing: 'What Western religions seem to have left out of their teachings is the experiential part for understanding, the opportunity for

experiencing myself, so that I may experience the cosmos and the difference between me and you' (1988: 230).

To have an experience that feels holy or spiritual is important to many
people, whether it occurs in a therapeutic context, in meditation, in
nature, in a New Age gathering or wherever. I have elsewhere (West,
1995c) explored the parallels between person-centred therapy and
Quakerism in Britain. These include a deep listening to what the other
person has to say without judging them, an acceptance and valuing of
silence, a valuing of (inner) experiencing, an ability to wait for words to
come including the use of inspiration, and a trust in the process that is
unfolding which for Quakers is seen as spiritual. The big difference is that
Quakers feel themselves to be explicitly spiritually guided to speak.

This sense of the link between therapy and New Age Spirituality was
also found among the respondents to my research into therapy and healing
(West, 1995a). I found that many of my respondents met their spiritual
and religious needs through unorthodox spiritual or healing groups rather
than through conventional religion. I was told:

> I'm a lapsed Catholic. I believe in all sorts of things like reincarnation, because
> I've had experiences.

> I'm not religious, but I am quite spiritual.

> I've practised meditation, it has deepened my connection with my inner and
> higher self.

Similar results have been found in studies of Californian therapists.
Shafranske and Malony (1985) discovered that 71 per cent of the Californian psychologists in their study considered spirituality to be personally
relevant but only 9 per cent reported a high level of involvement with
traditional religion. A further study they undertook (1990) found that over
half of the 409 psychologists who responded, as previously mentioned,
regarded their spirituality as an 'alternative spiritual path which is not part of
organized religion' (1990: 74).

The value of New Age Spirituality lies in its focus on the individual and
his or her own experience of their spirituality. The downside is that of
reinventing the wheel, and of the possibility of a shallow self-centred
approach to spirituality. However, there are clear elements of heretical
Christianity (e.g. the Christian quality of *A Course in Miracles*, Foundation
for Inner Peace, 1975 which is a popular self-help book for spiritual
growth) as well as elements from Buddhism other Eastern religions, and
paganism. We are in a time of great changes and uncertainties, in a time
when many people find traditional religions outdated and irrelevant. Not
surprisingly New Age Spirituality, with its eclectic approach and its focus
on and valuing of the individual and their experiences, is gaining in
popularity.

Therapy, regretfully, has become like a religion or a substitute for
religion for some people. Indeed at least one of my Quaker researchees

(West, 1998a) saw her faith and her transpersonal therapy work as insepar-able: it felt as if her psychosynthesis was her faith and her therapeutic work was her Quakerism, which I found disturbing, a blurring of the boundaries involved.

However, it is of crucial importance that issues relating to New Age Spirituality, to other religions and to the individual's spiritual life in general should be safely explorable within the psychotherapeutic relationship should the client so wish it.

DO-IT-YOURSELF SPIRITUALITY

Do-it-yourself or DIY spirituality is a phrase that is often used alongside or instead of New Age Spirituality. Professional theologians can be sneeringly dismissive of what they regard as 'do-it-yourself spirituality' or 'pick-and-mix religion'. This ignores the self-evident truth that all religion is humanly constructed. This includes even the Bible which was carefully and politically edited to suit the needs of the powers that be at that time – namely the Roman Empire. Maybe the Bible does consist of the word of God, but the choice of which words were to be included, and which not, was unlikely to have been merely a spiritual act. Indeed Christianity is a prime example of how a religion evolves and develops within its culture. For example the pacificism of the early Church has largely been replaced by notions of 'just wars' and every army has its chaplains who accept the necessity of killing your enemy. Newer brands of Christianity have arisen since the Reformation and continue to arise when people have found the existing Churches unacceptable for their spiritual needs. Indeed one of the challenges facing Christianity is: can it adapt itself and become more relevant to people's lives in the late twentieth century?

John Heron in his book *Sacred Science* speaks of people who are part of what he calls a 'self-generating spiritual culture' and he offers three inter-related criteria by which to identify people who belong to this group:

1 They affirm their own original relation to the presence of creation, find spiritual authority within and do not project it outward onto teachers, traditions or texts.
2 They are alert to the hazards of defensive and offensive spirituality, in which unprocessed emotional distress distorts spiritual development, either by denying parts of one's nature, or by making inflated claims in order to manipulate others.
3 They are open to genuine dialogue about spiritual beliefs and to colla-borative decision-making about spiritual practices undertaken together. (1998: 3)

This is a clear statement of a high quality approach to inquiry into spirituality.

NEW RELIGIOUS MOVEMENTS

> The use of the term 'New Religious Movement' does not imply that a movement is good or bad, that it is true or false, or genuine or fraudulent. (Barker, 1989: 4)

New religious movements are new religious groups that have emerged since the 1950s in Britain. They are no longer just variations on the Judaeo-Christian traditions but reflect the changing nature of multicultural Britain and especially reflect immigration and missionary activities from the USA and Indian subcontinent. Barker, who is probably the leading academic expert on such groups, suggests that over one million people in Britain have been or are members of such groups (quoted in Northcott, 1992).

There are estimated to be over 500 such groups in Britain and Barker (1989) lists the 100 or so who are known to INFORM. Probably the best known of this list are: Aetherius Society, Children of God, Church of Scientology, Divine Light Mission, human potential movement, International Society for Krishna Consciousness, neo-paganism, New Age movement, Nichiren Shoshu Buddhism, occultism, raja yoga, Rajneeshism, Rastafarianism, shamanism, Subud, transcendental meditation, transpersonal psychology, Unification Church, Wicca, witchcraft.

One can argue about who is included or excluded from this list, and I am certainly of the opinion that human potential movement and transpersonal psychology do not belong. Nevertheless this list does represent a range of spiritual and religious groups, a number of which have achieved some notoriety. Such groups are often labelled as 'cults' which does however have negative connotations. Wilson (1981) suggests that new religious movements have the following features:

> exotic provenance; new cultural life-style; a level of engagement markedly different from that of traditional Church Christianity; charismatic leadership; a following predominantly young and drawn in disproportionate measure from the better-educated and middle class sections of society; social conspicuity; international operation; and emergence within the last decade and a half. (quoted in Barker, 1989)

Not all new religious movements will fit all of Wilson's criteria, although membership of the better known ones is disproportionately middle or upper-middle class, with the exception of Rastafarians.

Fielding and Llewelyn suggest that members of what they call 'cults' typically:

1   adhere to a consensual belief system which is deviant in at least some particular with respect to the dominant cultural context;
2   sustain a high level of within-group cohesiveness, and reject participation in the majority culture;
3   are strongly influenced by group behavioural norms (that is, are conformist);

4 impute charismatic (or divine) power to the group or its leadership; and
5 are deviant with respect to the dominant religion. (1996: 274)

They point out that not all groups fit these criteria but that the key issues of rejecting values and norms of the popular culture is a shared feature. They are of the opinion that new religious movements and therapies are in competition for the same group of people – 'young, affluent, and self questioning'. They point to some commonalities between therapy and cult conversion. These include persuasion on the part of therapist or cult recruiter and a willingness for the client or cult member to change their beliefs and behaviours: 'In effect, the therapist persuades the patient to become more like the therapist' (1996: 278).

Heelas and Kohn (1996) maintain that a number of new religious movements owe their origins to the spirituality inherent in secular psychotherapy. They point to the spirituality that emerged from Rogerian therapy, Reichian therapy and psychodrama. They cite what they call self-religions like est and the followers of Bhagwan, both of which draw on Western therapeutic techniques and also put forward a form of Eastern spirituality, and they insist: 'A conservative guess would be that at least ten million Americans are currently involved with psychospiritual paths, ranging from spiritually significant encounter groups to fully-fledged self religions' (1996: 299).

Fielding and Llewelyn (1996) suggest that any psychological critic or supporter of new religious movements should be clear about the ethics and values that underpin their own position, and point out that ethical challenges made to new religious movements can be made against many psychological treatments.

Many new religious movements largely consist of first-generation believers, that is of converts. Such groups tend to be more enthusiastic, expounding simple truths, passionate, caring and immediate. They make big demands of time and commitment on their members who tend to be young, typically in their 20s, as is often the leadership of such groups. There is a high turnover in membership and over time the new religious group will tend to become more institutionalized.

New religious groups tend to have charismatic leaders:

New Religions are rarely initiated by a committee. Although sects may be formed by a group of dissatisfied persons breaking away from a larger body, several of the movements have, or have had, a founder or leader who is believed to have some special powers or knowledge, and whom his (or occasionally, her) followers are expected to believe and obey without question. (Barker, 1989: 13)

Such charismatic leaders have often, like shamans (see Chapter 1), undergone an initiatory illness or breakdown that led them to a point of new insight or revelation of the truth. As mentioned in Chapter 1, Ellenberger (1970) is of the opinion that both Freud and Jung suffered such illnesses before the maturing of their theories.

Benefits of membership of new religious movements are needless to say a source of controversy. Such groups are often accepting of mystical, spiritual or other 'strange' experiences or altered states of consciousness. Indeed, some of the groups offer such experiences via meditative and other practices. Also claimed as a benefit of membership includes career success, belonging to a community, self-development, spiritual teachings and bettering the world.

Whatever view one takes of such groups they seem here to stay, or rather new religious groups of one kind and another will always be created in response to existing and changing human circumstances. Such a process may well increase as the millennium approaches.

In the context of New Age Spirituality and new religious movements it is important to acknowledge the significance of paganism and its enduring influence on emerging notions of spirituality and the spiritual life. Paganism, despite its bad press from Christianity over the centuries, continues to flourish. It is claimed to be the fastest growing religion in Britain (Seymour, 1998). Paganism has its roots in the old religions of Europe. It honours the divine in humans and in nature. Its influence is apparent within Celtic Christianity and within traditional or shamanic forms of healing.

It would not be appropriate to end this discussion of New Age Spirituality and new religious movements without mentioning my own involvement in this whole area in the 1980s. My work in the early 1980s as a humanistic therapist was focused very much around my training as a Reichian therapist. Reichian therapy is derived from the work of Wilhelm Reich (1897–1957) who was a pupil of Freud's in the 1920s before breaking away. Reich believed that Freud's concept of the libido was the key to therapeutic work and he renamed this as orgone energy. His therapeutic work can be seen in terms of freeing the flow of orgone energy within the body.

Reich later discovered that this orgone energy was not just in all living things but also universally present in varying quantities. This might seem a strange idea, or certainly did in the 1930s and 1940s, but the idea of a life that is also universally presented has been a common feature of many Eastern philosophies and forms of medicine for centuries, for instance the notions of Chi energies in Tai Chi, or prana in yoga, or the energy in acupuncture, and so on. One of the little known side effects of Reichian therapy is that it can release latent psychic abilities. During 1981–2 I had several strange experiences that including seeing auras or colours around people, and sorting out these experiences led me reluctantly to become a spiritual healer (for a more detailed story see West, 1998b).

So I was now living in a universe that was alive with spiritual energies. My religious readings of the 1970s had somehow prepared me to view this in a very spiritual way but I could not reconcile my experiences with mainstream Christianity even though I felt the need for a spiritual home. It felt in some way as if every therapy or healing group that I was a member of, as either leader or participant, was itself in some way my spiritual group. Psychic and spiritual experiences of one kind or another were common in these groups, and outside the group sessions there were times set aside for meditation. I joined various meditation groups that met to focus healing energies for individuals or communities. Other rituals were developed in healing groups or offered separately. During the 1980s I would have described myself spiritually as New Age if asked.

Many of my friends in 1981 and 1982 became followers of Bhagwan Shree Rajneesh (as did one of my earliest humanistic trainers in 1974 plus many of her colleagues) and adopted orange clothing and Indian spiritual names. Although I was tempted, for I envied their belonging and their joy and mutual support, I could never bow down to any guru or leader. So I could not follow them. I knew my own path was English, within English culture in some way. I was in some sense in flight from my Englishness but unable to reconcile myself with our patriarchal heritage that included a Church of England that would not honour women or accept gays and lesbians.

In 1991 just before the Gulf War started I found myself by accident at a Quaker meeting. In the silence of the Quaker meeting I found the same spiritual energies that I had been exploring during the 1980s. An official statement was then read out about the approaching Gulf War which echoed my own unease at how we were rushing towards an armed conflict. Here was a group of peace makers who honoured women and welcomed gays and lesbians into their ranks, who were based on inner spiritual light and experience and had been around for 350 years. I felt a deep sense of arriving spiritually home after 25 years in the wilderness.

In this chapter we have seen that conventional Christianity is in decline in Britain. We can recognize and acknowledge the appeal of New Age Spirituality, the new religious movements, charismatic and fundamentalist Christianity and other faiths. People continue to have religious experiences in large numbers. This context of religious and spiritual change and ferment is the backdrop against which clients' spiritual issues will be manifest in psychotherapy.

This chapter has been a thumbnail sketch of some of the changing features of the spiritual and religious landscape in Britain today which will have relevance to the practice of psychotherapy. It is probably impossible to keep fully up to date with all developments, and in any case there is no substitute for listening to how clients in psychotherapy experience religion themselves.

5

The Spiritual Space and Spiritual Unfolding

In this chapter I will be exploring how the therapeutic space can be experienced as spiritual. I will draw on my own researches and experiences of spirituality and psychotherapy as well as those mentioned in the literature. It begins with a consideration of spiritual experiences in therapy, followed by a consideration of the spiritual space in therapy including groups.

SPIRITUAL EXPERIENCES IN THERAPY

In my research (West, 1995a; 1997) into therapists whose work includes healing there were a number of examples of spiritual experiences occurring in therapy sessions. A Gestalt psychotherapist described an experience that occurred during the course of one of his regular clients' therapy which he saw as representing a 'quantum leap' in that client's therapeutic process. Usually the therapeutic work with this client was fairly mundane. This time things were different from before the client even arrived. The therapist commented:

> I don't think I've ever experienced anything quite like it; it was just a totally different level of functioning of consciousness for us . . . It started before he arrived. I started to become aware of a sort of great calmness and a sort of contentment and peacefulness. He arrived, and we went into the therapy room and very quickly the room was filled with an incredible sort of soothing energy, totally undemanding energy.

This was experienced as healing by both client and therapist, and perhaps more importantly the client went on to make 'momentous decisions' about his life during that same therapy session.

Another respondent understood this sense of being part of something bigger than himself and his client in terms of resonance of the aura or energy field of himself and his client:

> When a certain level of resonance is achieved something comes in. It's a little bit like if you wanted to describe the mechanics or the dynamics behind the phrase 'when two or more are gathered together in my name'. If you take that phrase and the implication of that – when two people are in resonance, when

Table 5.1   *Healing phenomena in respondents' work*

Healing phenomena	Respondents no.	(n = 27) %
Healing energies present	23	86
Feeling part of something bigger than you and your client	21	78
Hands-on healing	20	74
Spiritual counselling	16	59
Feeling grace is present	15	56
Feeling God is present	10	37
Aura work	10	37
Spirit guides	8	30
Non-corporeal presences	8	30
Seeing auras	6	22
Channelling	6	22

there is a common purpose and there is something of a common field, and there is harmony there – I do think that there is often at that moment something else, something of the 'other' comes in at that point. That is my experience, that suddenly there is more than just two people in the room. Now whether that's grace, whether that's insight, whether that's healing, it depends on your language. It's certainly a qualitative difference, and I see that in the client, and at some point after that moment, I will probably draw their attention to it . . . When you are talking about the grace coming in, we [therapist and client] both get something from it, but that's not my energy, but it's my skill or my craft is to somehow bring us, this field we are in, this therapy, to the point where that can happen.

Fiona Moore (personal communication, 1999), on reading the above, commented: 'Practitioners who consciously seek to develop and refine their awareness of their own field and those of their clients can deliberately modify their field to establish a resonance with clients in order to enhance therapeutic effectiveness.'

Of the 30 people interviewed for this research, 27 filled in a follow-up questionnaire. One set of questions focused on healing phenomena and the results are summarized in Table 5.1. Over three-quarters reported feeling part of something bigger than themselves and their clients from time to time in their therapy work:

I'm very aware that when I'm with clients, there's a third party present, if you like. It's very difficult to explain, but I'm just aware of an other that makes sense and helps what's going on.

There was a sense of being with another person within a context which was now somehow very much greater.

This last respondent was convinced that this new development in his work was at least in part due to:

A very much greater deepening of my relationship with the essential core of my own being, or putting it theologically, to encounter God within.

Over half of the respondents were willing to say that they felt grace was present, and just over a third felt that God was present. Clearly my respondents were not a typical group of therapists since they replied to my requests for those willing to discuss healing phenomena in their work. However, I suspect this sense of feeling part of something bigger than oneself and one's client is quite common and inevitably those of a religious disposition may be drawn to speaking of God, the Goddess, grace or some other religious term.

It is possible, as I explored in Chapter 2, to view such experiences within the terms of Martin Buber's I–Thou relationship. It is also possible to view such therapeutic mergers with one's clients in non-spiritual terms. This view has been put forward by Alvin Mahrer (1978; 1993) with his concept of transformational psychology during which the therapist and client merge and share their experiencing. In this process 'to some extent the therapist's identity (personhood, self) becomes coterminal with that of the patient' (1978: 387). Carl Rogers advocated empathy as one of his three core conditions that therapists need to embody in their work. Rogers always added a rider, a limit to such empathy: 'to sense the client's private world as if it were your own, but without ever losing the *as if* quality' (Kirschenbaum and Henderson, 1990a: 226).

Mahrer, however, insists that his transformational psychology goes beyond empathy, and indeed seems to lose this 'as if' boundary: 'Instead of being empathic with the person, you are fully being the person. Instead of knowing the person's world, you are living it' (1993: 34).

Various authors have written about spirituality and therapy, many of whom are referred to elsewhere in this book, especially in Chapters 1 and 2. Brian Thorne, perhaps Britain's leading person-centred therapist, has particularly written on this topic. His chapter 'The quality of tenderness' (Thorne, 1991) especially captures his understanding of those moments in therapy when the therapeutic encounter becomes a spiritual experience for both parties. He says of tenderness:

> In the first place it is a quality which irradiates the total person – it is evident in the voice, the eyes, the hands, the thoughts, the feelings, the beliefs, the moral stance, the attitude to things animate and inanimate, seen and unseen. Secondly, it communicates through its responsive vulnerability that suffering and healing are interwoven. Thirdly, it demonstrates a preparedness and an ability to move between the worlds of the physical, the emotional, the cognitive and the mystical without strain. Fourthly, it is without shame because it is experienced as the joyful embracing of the desire to love and is therefore a law unto itself. Fifthly, it is a quality which transcends the male and the female but is never-theless nourished by the attraction of the one for the other in the quest for wholeness. (1991: 76)

Notice that Brian Thorne uses the word 'mystical' and describes an ability to move in and out of the mystical world. The notion of becoming a law unto itself has ethical implications which will be discussed further later. So how does Brian Thorne experience this 'tenderness'?

> I feel in touch with myself to the extent that it is not an effort to think or know what I am feeling. It is as if energy is flowing through me and I am simply allowing it free passage. I feel a physical vibrancy and this often has a sexual component and a stirring in the genitals. I feel powerful and yet at the same time almost irrelevant. My client seems more accurately in focus: he or she stands out in sharp relief from the surrounding décor. When he or she speaks, the words belong uniquely to him or her. Physical movements are a further confirmation of uniqueness. It seems as if for a space, however brief, two human beings are fully alive because they have given themselves and each other permission to risk being fully alive. At such moments I have no hesitation in saying that my client and I are caught up in a stream of love. Within this stream there comes an effortless or intuitive understanding and what is astonishing is how complex this understanding can be. (1991: 77)

Much of what Brian Thorne says in the above quote matches classic descriptions of the mystical state including heightened awareness and emotional state, even the sexual stirring. Thorne (1991; 1998) has written about the medieval Christian mystic Julian of Norwich as 'the most stunning avant-garde theologian I have ever stumbled on' and he has suggested that she could be considered as the patron saint of counselling. Brian Thorne directs a counsellor training course at the University of East Anglia that includes an explicit spiritual component.

Brian Thorne also speaks of the joy involved for him and his client in these moments of tenderness: 'There may be an overwhelming desire for physical contact which can result in holding hands or in a close embrace. There may be an urgent need to talk about death or God or the soul' (1991: 77). Brian Thorne asks how we can trust such experiences; he comments that it is as if 'joy and knowledge are forbidden fruits' (1991: 71), and he acknowledges that some people see it as the work of the Devil.

Needless to say Brian Thorne has become the subject of great controversy within the therapy world, not merely for his recognition and valuing of our spirituality but also for his case study of his work with a client he called Sally (Thorne, 1991). I will not repeat all of the issues and debate about this but will merely note that Thorne appears to be breaking the current British Association for Counselling (BAC) guidelines since he describes working with his client in her room at a conference for an extended therapy session and he also speaks of holding her in a naked embrace. In his defence he maintains that his work with Sally occurred long before the BAC guidelines were first introduced. Perhaps in the late 1990s we therapists are taking a very cautious approach to how we work with clients.

This case highlights the need for very clear boundaries with work involving our client's spirituality where they may often be exploring unbounded experiences. (See the ethical discussion in Chapter 9.) Also person-centred counsellors and psychotherapists (and humanistic therapists in general) often seem to underestimate the power relationship between client and therapist, a point made clear by Martin Buber in his dialogue with Carl Rogers explored in Chapter 2, namely that the therapist is healthy and there to support the client who has a problem. So however much the therapist works to empower the client, the therapist will still have the greater power. Therapists inevitably have greater experience than clients of what psychotherapy is and what it entails. Morally therapists have to ensure their clients' safety and behave impeccably towards them.

Fiona Moore (personal communication, 1999) suggests that if therapists are seeking to enable a spiritual space to be available to their clients then this itself introduces the possibility of the unexpected occurring. As she comments: 'discernment is paramount here and so too is the skill and experience of the practitioner'.

SPIRITUAL SPACE

As part of my research into therapists whose work includes healing I set up a human inquiry group (West, 1996) with myself and six of my respondents. This group met for four weekends to explore therapy and healing. One of the key outcomes of this group was the concept that the therapeutic space can be seen as a spiritual space: that the therapists can hold in their mind that the therapy space is spiritual, and that this will allow the client to explore their spirituality and spiritual issues if they so wish. As one group member put it: 'Space is where the spirit is. Space is where we get out of the way and allow whatever we may call it, God's spirit, whatever, to be. That's like a healing because we are not interfering, allowing whatever it is to happen.'

The importance of holding such a space for clients, a space of not using technique, a space that is seen as spiritual, was not lost on the group. One member commented: 'In the work that I do I actually see it as beyond the psyche . . . [I find] there's spiritual in the sense of spiritual phenomena and there's spiritual in the sense of going beyond the psyche into the soul.'

It was clear to the group that such soulwork depends on the spiritual development of the therapist involved. I commented at that time: 'If you engage with the soul level of your client, you have to first engage with your own soul in some sense.' Another member was moved to add: 'Unless you keep some spiritual dimension in your mind as you're dealing with the client, the client is not going to transcend his or her normal self.'

This notion of a spiritual space was one of the key concepts that emerged from the group as a result of its experiences, and it is not surprising perhaps to discover that a similar concept emerged from an earlier human inquiry group into whole person medical practice initiated by Peter Reason and John Heron (Heron and Reason, 1985; Reason, 1988). A subgroup of their human inquiry group was established to

Box 5.1   *Founding statement of the PsychoSpiritual Initiative*

We are a small network of therapists and healers with a shared spiritual understanding meeting regularly in London, now offering as a group a healing space to others for exploration, development, supervision and support.

explore spirituality and a report was produced listing 17 principles, one of which was the metaphor of 'spiritual spaces'.

They suggest these 'spiritual spaces' could be viewed in two possible ways. Firstly, they could be seen as gaps or openings in the interaction with the client in which the psychic and/or spiritual is latent or tacitly present, and could be made explicit by some spiritual intervention. Secondly, they could refer to openings or spaces between ordinary and extraordinary reality that could be created by appropriate rituals or ceremonies, or merely noticed when they occurred spontaneously.

This similarity between this view of 'spiritual spaces' and my group's use of spiritual space is apparent, though in this case it is seen not as a metaphor but as a reality, something that can be experienced, a space that is felt, and felt as being spiritual. My group continues to meet quarterly under the title PsychoSpiritual Initiative and it offers the spiritual space to all who might benefit from it. Its founding statement is shown in Box 5.1.

To explore this matter further I will attempt to describe how a typical PsychoSpiritual Initiative or PSI consultation develops. A would-be visitor to PSI will have made telephone contact with one of its members, who will explain something of what it offers and help the would-be visitor determine whether a consultation would be helpful for them. If so a time is arranged for them to consult with the group during one of its regular weekend meetings. The PSI group currently consists of seven members, three men and four women, who each intend to be present at the regular quarterly weekend meetings.

When the visitor arrives they are welcomed and brief introductions are made before an opening meditation is held. This will usually involve some words being said, possibly meditative music, as well as a short period of silence. During this meditation it is very likely that images, thoughts, healing and therapeutic insights will be occurring to members of PSI. The visitor is then invited to say something of what brings them to consult PSI. From then on the process varies. It is likely that PSI members will draw on the images and insights that arose during the meditation and afterwards, and this can occasionally result in healing, aura work being given, or a specific meditation or guided fantasy being offered to the visitor. Counselling of an intuitive and spiritual nature will also very likely result, again often inspired by images and insight arising.

Visitors are often on a spiritual path and find what PSI offers them to be welcome and relevant to their own development. A number of visitors comment immediately when they enter the room in which the PSI group is gathered on the 'atmosphere' and how good it feels. Following the period of counsel a further meditation is used as a closing ritual which can include a prayer, meditative music and a further short period of silence.

Visitors are invited to give the PSI group feedback which usually follows in the form of a letter within a few days of the consultation. Inevitably the experience of consulting with the PSI group has proved powerful and of great value. Occasionally, there will be useful and critical feedback that helps the fine tuning of this largely intuitive process.

The importance of the therapist regarding the therapy room as a place where the client's spirituality is present becomes clear if we reflect on David Hay's findings discussed in Chapter 1, when he speaks of the taboo that exists for people in talking about such experiences and of the difficulties people have in finding appropriate language to discuss such experiences. These findings were replicated in my research into therapy and healing (West, 1995a; 1997). Consequently it is important that therapists communicate a clear acceptance of spirituality and spiritual experiences in order to help their clients overcome this taboo.

THE SPIRITUAL SPACE WITHIN GROUPS

I have been aware recently in a number of group settings, sometimes with therapists, sometimes not, that a spiritual space has become available. Within this context I have noticed how people are enabled to share deeply about their spirituality in a way that is very transforming; perhaps being able to break the taboo on talking about spiritual experiences is crucial.

This seems to have a sense of what Jung (1967) called 'synchronicity' about it. Over a number of months I was confronted with various experiences in which this 'spiritual space' appeared to be present to such an extent that I had to take heed of it. (Of course to be strictly true to Jung's definition such events should occur simultaneously.) It certainly was, and remains, a regular feature of the PsychoSpiritual Initiative group mentioned above. However, I took this rather as a matter of fact and assumed it was fairly unique to that group. I then had the opportunity of working with a group of second year Advanced Diploma in Counselling students on spirituality and counselling. I suggested to this group of six students that instead of my inputting all sorts of information on spirituality, we shared what the topic meant to us and see where that took us. Unexpectedly (for me) a deep sharing resulted which continued over the four afternoon meetings of this group. There was a deep personal sharing around spirituality, a sharing of dilemmas from members' counselling work, and plenty of exploring of theoretical issues and the passing on of practical information. Besides this there were often periods of reflective silence out of which rather naturally would emerge a new thread of sharing.

Soon after this I joined a small Quaker group that met monthly to explore and share its members' spiritual journeying. This group began each session with the traditional time of Quakerly silence out of which arose spontaneous sharing by group members around the pre-selected theme of the evening. Such themes were pain, suffering, healing, hope, despair etc. The group has proved to be one of the deepest spiritual spaces I have entered. Some very personal sharing has occurred which has had a deep impact on those present and which is reminiscent of Carl Rogers's view that 'what is most personal and unique in each of us . . . if it were shared or expressed, speaks most deeply to others' (in Kirschenbaum and Henderson, 1990a: 27). Occasionally in this group the thread gets lost, and the group drifts off into everyday conversation. At such times I wonder if the group, or perhaps one of its members, can only stay with the deep sharing for a limited period.

Then occurred another apparent synchronicity. As I gradually became aware of this phenomenon I conceived of co-running a course that would lie somewhere at the meeting point between a therapy group and a spiritual retreat with a focus on the concept of spiritual unfolding. I immediately realized who my co-facilitator should be and wrote to her accordingly with a draft version of what the group would be about. A couple of months later at a meeting of the Quaker group one of its members spoke of his sense of his spiritual development in words that were eerily similar, if not identical, to my own words. This I had to take note of, and the group that had been merely a good idea up to that point became a concrete reality. The final version of the main text for the leaflet promoting this group, as devised by myself and my co-facilitator Mary Swale, is shown in Box 5.2.

This spiritual unfolding which results when the spiritual space is established has a considerably different feel from how a counselling or psychotherapy group will usually be experienced. Much of what happens for people occurs in the silences, and is not always shared there and then. The effects for group members can be experienced as very subtle and on occasions it takes several weeks for the full effect to be realized.

Reflecting on my experiences of the spiritual space, there appear to be several key features that make such experiences possible:

1 Acceptance that the space is a spiritual space.
2 Ability to tolerate silence so that the spiritual space can unfold.
3 Ability to listen to one another in a deep and holistic sense, without composing a reply.
4 Willingness to speak authentically.
5 Acceptance of the experience(s) that occurs (such experiences are likely to be referred to as spiritual).

If these features are in place at least to a minimal extent, an unfolding that is experienced as spiritual will occur.

The concept of the spiritual space has profound implications for the training, practice and supervision of therapists as explored in Chapter 7. Perhaps the most overriding question is: how far can I be present to my client's, trainee's or supervisee's reality, including their spirituality? This is

Box 5.2   *Spiritual unfolding group description*

The purpose of this group is to help its members in the spiritual unfolding
which is at work within them and their worlds. This unfolding can take
unique and often unexpected forms for each of us. For some it may be a new
insight, for others a change of energy or a release of feelings. Some may be
moved on by their dreams or by facing a difficult life decision. For others
unfolding will occur in the silence of their hearts.

This will be neither a therapy group nor a retreat as such, although silence
will play a key part in the process and it is hoped that participants will
experience times of inner change and healing during the course of the
weekend.

The Nature of the Group
Spirit can be experienced as an unfolding process at the heart of our lives,
inherent in us and our world, a part of us that goes deeper than any religious
belief or lack of it. This unfolding, which seems to occur within each person,
feels satisfying and usually benefits us and those around us. However, it can
sometimes seem to go too fast or too slow, or become blocked or mis-
directed. It may then feel painful and sometimes even frightening.

The group will aim to foster safe and supported unfolding within its members.
We will offer a framework for the weekend, to include structured quiet time,
time for meditation or other spiritual practice, and time for sharing experiences in the group or in pairs. We will also allow free space for rest and
spontaneous unfolding! Intuition on the part of all group members will play a
key role in what happens.

We ask you to come with a clear intention to use the weekend to look more
deeply into your spiritual life, and a willingness to participate in the group.
We hope you will bring both your wisdom and what obscures it – your
darkness and your light – so that we can all be enriched by sharing these. We
undertake to contain and focus the group, to encourage a quality of space in
which each of us can feel safe to explore together and be open with each
other. You will not, however, be pressurized by us to share more than feels
right for you.

only possible if I am at peace with the notion of spirituality. It is not
necessary to be religious, or even to label the phenomena discussed above
as 'spiritual'. It is necessary to be open to our clients', supervisees' and
trainees' experiences and the language they choose to discuss such
experiences. Otherwise it is likely that people will be inhibited, the taboo
against discussing spirituality will remain in place, and we will be able to
say all too easily, 'My clients never talk about spirituality.'

6

Meeting the Challenge: Necessary Knowledge

In this chapter I will be exploring how therapists can prepare themselves for working with their clients' spiritual issues, and in the following chapter the implications this approach has for the therapeutic encounter. I am concerned here with some of the information, experience and awareness necessary on the part of the therapist so that she or he can be open to clients' spirituality as it manifests within the therapeutic encounter. This chapter includes a consideration of spiritual awakening and emergence; assessment issues including spiritual assessment; spiritual addictions; countertransference matters; spiritual development of therapists; mapping the psychospiritual; and the possibilities offered by a phenomenological-existential view of therapy and spirituality.

SPIRITUAL AWAKENING AND EMERGENCE

Some spiritual or mystical experiences are one-off isolated events whose effects for the person involved wear off over time. However, some spiritual experiences have a deep and lasting impact on the person concerned such that they may be referred to as spiritual awakenings or spiritual emergence. Assagioli (1986), the founder of the transpersonal approach called psychosynthesis, suggests that there are four critical stages in a person's spiritual development or awakening:

1 Crises preceding the spiritual awakening.
2 Crises caused by the spiritual awakening.
3 Reactions following the spiritual awakening.
4 Phases of 'the process of transmutation' of the personality in which higher or more spiritual levels of self-realization can be achieved.

Assagioli maintained that more and more people are now experiencing spiritual awakenings, although this is only based on anecdotal evidence, albeit increasingly reported. The same claim is made by Grof and Grof (1989) who offer an expanded view of spiritual awakening which they call spiritual emergence or spiritual emergency. They delineate 10 forms of spiritual emergency:

1 *Shamanic crisis* The process, often an illness, by which someone becomes a shaman. There is understanding and support and training available in societies where shamanic crisis occurs but in Western societies such experiences are likely to be misdiagnosed.

2 *Awakening of Kundalini* The serpent or spiritual energy that resides in a latent form at the base of the spine. Some yogic practices aim to awaken and release this energy which can also occur spontaneously. It needs careful handling when awakening.

3 *Episodes of unitive consciousness ('peak experiences')* An experience akin to a spiritual experience in which one feels at one with all of creation.

4 *Psychological renewal through return to the centre* An extreme form of the Jungian process of individuation by which a person truly becomes a separate being, in this case through an inner battle and visionary states.

5 *The crisis of psychic opening* An increase in intuitive abilities is common in any form of spiritual awakening. However, in this case the abilities increase dramatically and confusingly and can include precognition, telepathy and clairvoyance. Out-of-body experiences are also possible in which one's consciousness appears to separate from one's body which can then be viewed from afar.

6 *Past-life experiences* Becoming aware of the idea that one has lived previous lives which may involve people and places in one's current life and seem to explain otherwise inexplicable familiarities and possible difficulties with people.

7 *Communication with spirit guides or channelling* A spirit guide is a particular spiritual entity that takes an interest in an individual and offers her or him useful information. If such information is passed on directly to others it is usually called 'channelling'.

8 *Near-death experiences* Such experiences are now being increasingly reported, especially by people having serious accidents or surgery. Many report walking along a tunnel towards a white light and meeting spirit beings including dead friends and relatives and then having to return reluctantly to one's body which is often viewed from outside. After such an experience people often report losing a fear of dying and their lives can change quite dramatically (Moody, 1975).

9 *Experiences of close encounters with UFOs* 'The experience of encounters with and abduction by what appears to be extraterrestrial spacecraft or beings can often precipitate serious emotional and intellectual crises that have much in common with spiritual emergencies' (Grof and Grof, 1989: 23).

10 *Possession states* Grof and Grof (1989) regard instances of possession – when a person feels invaded in some way by an outside entity – as being a spiritual crisis and not something to respond to with fear.

The experience of going beyond our ordinary sense of self into the transpersonal realm or into an altered state of consciousness is often seen as healing (Vaughan, 1986). However, Vaughan (1991) contends that there can be a 'shadow' side to a person's spiritual quest (explored later in this chapter), involving what she calls 'spiritual addiction' based on 'wishful thinking and the abdication of personal responsibility'. She suggests that this is why some psychotherapists view spirituality as 'pathological'. She also states that spiritual practices are no substitute for confronting problems, although it could be maintained that authentic spiritual practice would address real difficulties with living. Wilber (1980) offers us a different view when he suggests that we can have both pre-personal experiences (that is regressive experiences to childhood and perhaps earlier) and transpersonal experiences. He maintains that we should not confuse the two.

However, I do not believe that it is the role of the therapist to deny that the client's spiritual experience is genuine. That experience is for the client to work with and make sense of, perhaps with the support of the therapist. Carlat suggests we follow the approach of the anthropologist Obeyesekere (1984) in interpreting but not reducing spiritual and religious experiences, so that 'when an individual is allowed to elaborate her spiritual experiences without encountering a skeptical response, she may develop insight into the psychological meaning of her quest' (Carlat, 1989: 148). This is effectively a phenomenological viewpoint which is explored later in this chapter. Carlat is of course assuming that the psychological is the wider frame from within which to view the experience rather than using a spiritual framework within which to understand the experience, which is the criticism John Rowan (1993) makes of Jung, discussed in Chapter 2.

ASSESSMENT ISSUES

It is my belief that the key assessment question to ask myself and my would-be client during the initial counselling session is: can we work together? How we actually assess clients is a complex issue. My own impression of what happens when I assess a client for therapy is that I draw upon my previous experience of working as a therapist but I also monitor my own inner reactions, thoughts and feelings about the client present in the room with me, my sense of what therapeutic work they are seeking to do with me, and whether both of us have the resources to do such work. This is a compact description of what has become a fairly intuitive process based on training, knowledge and previous experience.

Although I think that every therapist does in fact do some kind of assessment process, however informal, there are a number of therapists who do not do a formal assessment at the start of their client's therapy. I will not explore in great detail or repeat the many excellent writings that are emerging around counselling and psychotherapy assessment (see McLeod, 1998 for a useful discussion of this area) but I think it would be valuable here to focus on three aspects: the process of spiritual assessment proposed by Richards and Bergin (1997); specific issues raised around spirituality using Lukoff's (1985) proposed diagnostic tool of mystical experience with psychotic features as a useful framework; and issues relating to how healthy the client's spiritual attitudes are.

Richards and Bergin (1997) argue that there are compelling reasons why therapists should conduct a religious–spiritual assessment of their clients. These are:

1 That it will help therapists to better understand their clients' world views and thereby aid empathic understanding and sensitive therapeutic work.
2 That it enables the therapist to assess whether the client's religious-spiritual orientation is healthy or not and to determine its impact on their presenting problems.
3 That it helps determine whether the client's religious and spiritual beliefs and community can be a resource for healing.
4 That it enables the therapist to determine which if any spiritual interventions in therapy could be helpful to the client.
5 That it enables the therapist to determine whether the client has unresolved spiritual doubts, concerns or needs that should be addressed in their therapy.

Richards and Bergin (1997) present a multilevel model for assessment of clients as shown in Figure 6.1. Level 1 (the global assessment level) covers the kinds of basic questions that therapists need to have answered in order to decide whether therapy is appropriate for the client involved. Level 2 involves an in-depth assessment of those sectors which warrant further exploring. For example a client who reports good physical health at a level 1 assessment would not be further assessed physically at level 2. However, should they have cancer, further questions would arise about what treatment they were receiving, medication etc.

Richards and Bergin (1997) suggest that the level 1 spiritual assessment is of what they refer to as an ecumenical nature, which seeks to gain general information about the client's religious and spiritual views. They suggest therapists seek answers to the following questions:

1 What is the client's metaphysical world view?
2 What was the client's childhood religious affiliation and experiences?
3 What is the client's current religious affiliation and level of devoutness?
4 Does the client believe his or her spiritual beliefs and lifestyle are contributing to his or her presenting problems and concerns in any way?
5 Does the client have any religious and spiritual concerns and needs?
6 Is the client willing to explore his or her religious and spiritual issues and to participate in spiritual interventions?
7 Does the client perceive that his or her religious and spiritual beliefs and community are a potential source of strength and assistance?

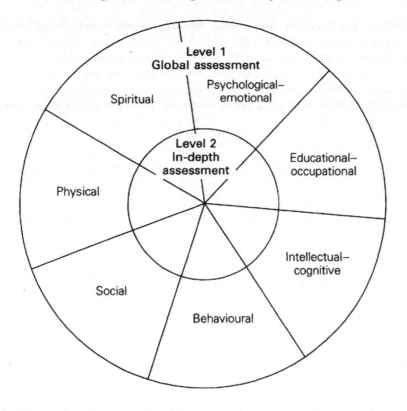

Figure 6.1 *A multilevel multidimensional assessment strategy (Richards and Bergin, 1997)*

Questions 2, 3 and 7 rather assume that the client does have a religious background, which may well not be the case in Britain. For clients who have a spiritual or religious world view which they feel is relevant to their problems and are willing to explore in therapy, a level 2 assessment is indicated. Richards and Bergin (1997) suggest questions of the following kind are useful:

1 How orthodox is the client? Within their own religious denomination?
2 What is the client's religious problem solving style (i.e. deferring, collaborative or self-directing)?
3 How does the client perceive God?
4 Does the client have a sound understanding of the important doctrines and teachings of his or her religious tradition?
5 Are the client's lifestyle and behaviour congruent with his or her religious and spiritual beliefs and values?
6 What stage of faith development is the client in? (See Fowler's, 1981 stages of faith.)

7 Does the client have a spiritual assurance of his or her eternal spiritual identity and divine worth?
8 Does the client feel a sense of spiritual well-being?
9 Is the client's religious orientation predominantly intrinsic, healthy, and mature?
10 In what ways, if any, are the client's religious and spiritual background, beliefs and lifestyle affecting his or her presenting problems and disturbance?

Richards and Bergin (1997) are open about the fact that they are writing within a Judaeo-Christian perspective which they maintain is the religious tradition of the vast majority of their fellow Americans. However, the questions listed above are consequently biased and would need to be modified to take account of those whose religious faith involved belief in more than one God or Goddess, or no God at all, or whose faith did not include eternal life.

This assessment process can itself be spiritually alive: 'For psychotherapists who believe that God can inspire and enlighten human beings, a religious and spiritual assessment will always be more than just gathering and conceptualizing information' (1997: 198). It can itself involve something akin to Buber's I–Thou encounter within which extra insight into the client's condition may well become available.

In Chapter 1 we considered the question of what is healthy spirituality and drew on the work of Allport in considering intrinsic and extrinsic religiosity. Besides the question of whether the client's religiosity and spirituality are of a healthy nature or not, the question arises as to whether the spiritual experiences they have and report are also healthy. However, discernment around spiritual experiences is not easy. As Laing states: 'Experience may be judged as invalidly mad or validly mystical . . . The distinction is not easy' (1967: 132).

Lukoff points to the assessment problems around diagnosing psychosis: 'The phenomenology (imagery, cognitions) of the psychotic condition share many characteristics with dream experiences . . . hallucinogenic drug trips . . . spiritual awakenings . . . near death experiences . . . and shamanic experiences' (1985: 162). Lukoff (1985) reminds us that psychoses and religious experiences have been linked together since time immemorial. Prophets in the Old Testament were seen as 'mad', and 'holy fools' were common in the Middle Ages. Psychiatric literature today discusses the similarity between psychotic symptoms and aspects of mystical experiences. David Hay (1982) points out that many people who have religious experiences do not discuss them for fear of being considered mad.

Lukoff (1985) provides us with a model which I suggest we can see as a spectrum with pure mystical experience at one end and pure psychosis at the other. In between we can have varying mixtures of mystical experience with psychotic features, or psychotic experience with mystical features. He also makes a useful distinction between temporary psychotic episodes and long-term psychosis. Temporary psychosis can lead to a better functioning individual in some cases as noted by Assagioli (1986), Ellenberger (1970), Grof and Grof (1989) and Laing (1972) among others.

Lukoff advises us that 'the content of an experience alone usually does not determine whether an individual is psychotic' (1985: 164). Of more importance is the difficulty psychotic individuals have in establishing a shared 'intersubjective reality' with others. However, this is partially due to what efforts if any are made to understand a possibly psychotic person's internal frame of reference. It is important to assess how capable such a person is in managing everyday life. Indeed, to Lukoff these last two points form a crucial part of a psychotic diagnosis.

Lukoff suggests five criteria which must all be present to define a mystical experience: ecstatic mood, which is probably the most common feature of mystical experiences; sense of newly gained knowledge including new insights into life; perceptual alterations, that is heightened sensations which may include auditory and visual hallucinations; delusions, which have themes related to mythology that include current cultural phenomena; and no conceptual disorganization, that is no disruption of thoughts, incoherence or blocking. Lukoff suggests that there are eight themes commonly occurring in mystical experiences: death, rebirth, a journey, encounters with spirits, cosmic conflict, magical powers, new society and divine union.

He is able to put forward criteria which need to be present to predict which clients will have positive outcomes for psychotic episodes. At least two of the following four criteria need to be present:

1   Good pre-episode functioning.
2   Acute onset of symptoms over three months or less.
3   Stressful precursors to the episode, e.g. major life change or transition.
4   A positive exploratory attitude towards the experience which will facilitate successful integration of the experience.

All of this suggests the need for treatment of mystical experience with psychotic features by not immediately using medication to bring the person out of their psychosis. 'Unfortunately treatment methods utilizing expression and exploration of psychotic episodes have not been widely incorporated by mental health professionals in private practice or at treatment sites' (Lukoff, 1985: 176). Lukoff optimistically suggests that many people with mystical experience with psychotic features could be treated by their family and friends if 24-hour sanctuary could be provided. He suggests even people in prolonged psychosis with mystical features could be helped in non-hospital residential settings with medical support.

Pioneering work was done in Britain in this area by Laing and Cooper among others from the late 1960s onwards. They set up houses where 24-hour support was made available (see Laing, 1972; Cooper, 1970). A recent example of such an episode and how it was dealt with is described in the next chapter. However: 'To traditionally-trained mental health professionals, the proposition that some psychotic episodes are growthful may seem to be wishful thinking or even magical thinking' (Lukoff, 1985: 178).

It is worth noting that the fourth edition of the *Diagnostic and Statistical Manual of Mental Disorders* (DSM-IV: American Psychiatric Association, 1994) has a new section (V62.89) called 'Religious or Spiritual Problem':

> This category can be used when the focus of clinical attention is a religious or spiritual problem. Examples include distressing experiences that involve loss or questioning of faith, problems associated with conversion to a new faith, or questioning of spiritual values that may not necessarily be related to an organized church or religious institution. (1994: 685)

This is to be welcomed but clearly does not address all of the issues raised by mystical experiences with psychotic features, since there is no mention of spiritual or mystical experiences within it and it seems to lack the breadth of understanding of spirituality that is put forward in this book, namely that spirituality is a key or even the key component of our lives.

Allman et al.'s (1992) survey of therapists' attitudes to mystical experiences mentioned above showed some further interesting results. They provided respondents with a brief vignette or case study of a client having a mystical experience with some psychotic features. Some therapists considered the client psychotic regardless of the information presented; others seemed to ignore or discount the psychotic features and regarded the client as probably not psychotic. In other words it seemed as if the therapists' view of mystical experiences was biasing their responses. Therapists having had a mystical experience themselves, regarding their own spirituality as important and operating from a humanistic/existential approach, were more likely to view such experiences as healthy. It is apparent then that any client having a mystical experience and feeling sufficiently troubled by it will have a varying response from therapists, which I suspect holds true for Britain as well as the USA.

There is a deeper issue around assessment and diagnosis that deserves careful consideration. Our sense of reality is a cultural construct, indeed the differing schools of therapy are based on differing views of people. Once a new diagnostic category is devised, more and more people are suddenly diagnosed as fitting it and of course in need of treatment by the very therapists making the diagnosis (Gergen, 1996).

Gergen talks of diagnostics as a 'deficit discourse' and maintains:

> Diagnostics presumes that we could diagnose the problem, presumes that there is a problem, that exists in nature and it is our task to measure it as it is, so it begins with the reality of the problem. And now we try to develop a vocabulary that would precisely discriminate among various sorts of problems, thus the various phases of DSM . . . DSM is a byproduct of a community of therapists and psychiatrists by and large who read the world in those terms . . . In effect, the very idea of disease and mental disease and disorder is in some sense our terminology of our club – it's our local group, at this time in history, at this time in the culture. And to presume that we are measuring a thing in itself is a

dangerous enterprise. It is a political and social enterprise because as we do that measurement, as we objectify those categories, as we treat those as the real, and share those realities with those outside of the profession, share them with a culture – these terms, these distinctions become available to people in the local conditions to construct their lives in. They become the ways in which they understand their lives . . . So as we produce a discourse of disease, we also produce a society in which disease becomes the common way of understanding oneself. (1996: 4–5)

Gergen suggests that we replace this diagnostic deficit with dialogue, indeed abandon diagnosis and work towards alternative terminologies. It remains striking how many more women than men end up in mental hospitals, likewise how many black children get labelled educationally subnormal. It is too easy to pretend such diagnostics are culturally neutral.

In this context of questioning the value of diagnosis it is worth recalling Carl Rogers's criticism of diagnosis, in which he suggests that the only value he can find in diagnosis is that it may reassure the therapist so that they can work more effectively with their client. Rogers, acting congruently with his theories, advocated that therapists work in the same way with all clients, namely by offering the core conditions of positive unconditional regard, empathy and congruence. If the client perceived these conditions to be available then they would make therapeutic progress (Rogers, 1980).

In 1957 Rogers undertook a research programme that used client-centred therapy with hospitalized schizophrenic patients. The results of this study showed that a client-centred approach was not especially effective with such clients. The work had a huge impact on the team that worked with Rogers (McLeod, 1998). However, Rogers records among his lessons from this work the following:

> We have come to realize that almost none of the individuals with whom we have been working have ever affirmed themselves. They have never, in any meaningful way, said 'I feel', 'I live', 'I have a right to be'. They have instead been passive receivers of life's hurts, blows and events. It takes, in my experience, great patience to wait for the germination and budding of the will to say 'I am, I deserve to be'. (1962: 15)

SPIRITUAL ADDICTIONS

It is important that we do not assume that anyone and everyone engaged in following a spiritual path, or otherwise exploring their spirituality, is inevitably doing so in a healthy way. It is necessary to explore the meaning to our clients of their use of spirituality, of what part it plays in their lives. Frances Vaughan warns us of the dangers of what she calls 'spiritual addictions': 'Whenever spirituality is based on wishful thinking and the abdication of personal responsibility, it is potentially addictive' (1991: 106).

As an example of such addiction Vaughan refers to how some members of religious communities may be unable to survive on their own in the outside world. Also spiritually addicted are people who use spirituality as a 'magic solution to problems they are unwilling to face' (1991: 106). She suggests that this is perhaps why many psychologists and therapists pathologize spirituality or view it with suspicion, that is that they have come across too few examples of healthy spirituality.

Some people are drawn to spiritual practices for the wrong reasons. I have come across several earnest young men who develop an interest in spiritual and occult powers, clearly inflating their egos, and who give me a sense of having closed hearts and a lack of humility. Vaughan warns us of the danger of merely seeking a high through spiritual practices:

> In so far as one is attracted to altered states for the purpose of getting high and avoiding the pain of ordinary life, these states become addictive. It is natural, then, that these practices are attractive to people who are having difficulty with their personal lives. (1991: 107)

Spirituality then is not meant to be an avoidance of life, its problems and dilemmas. Indeed, there are strong arguments put forward within many religious traditions for the value of living an ordinary life and for facing up to human suffering and the human and spiritual growth that can then result. One of the apparent differences in our modern life is that spirituality has become a key area of interest to younger people. The older traditions, as recognized by Jung in his famous quote about the value of religion to those in the second part of their lives, suggested that the spiritual path was more for those whose families had grown up and who had the time and the inclination to pursue the spiritual life.

Vaughan warns us against people who deny their shadow and hence regard people from spiritual traditions other than their own as wrong and misguided: 'Sometimes people who call themselves spiritual are in fact bigoted, judgemental, and condemning of anyone who does not accept a particular dogma or belief system' (1991: 107). Feeling ourselves to be spiritually special is to be guarded against, for the spiritual can be, and is, to be found in the ordinary. Spirituality can be motivated by fear and guilt and can then be psychologically crippling. There is also the danger of idolatry, of focusing too exclusively on a narrow part of a religion or on the icons and ideals of that religion.

Thankfully Vaughan gives us some pointers towards healthy spirituality: 'First of all, psychologically healthy spirituality supports personal freedom, autonomy, and self-esteem, as well as social responsibility. It does not deny our humanity or depend on suppression or denial of emotions' (1991: 116). It is worth realizing that Vaughan writes as a US transpersonal therapist and that the values she supports above reflect this tradition. It can be argued that the depth of the spiritual path involves surrender to the divine and in some traditions to the religious teacher. Likewise, a spiritual journey may lead to a different relationship with one's emotions, not a denial but perhaps a transcendence, a dis-identification with one's emotions. This could be represented by a move away from 'I am what I feel' to 'I am and I experience myself as having feelings.'

Vaughan insists that a healthy spirituality potentially exists in everyone and is not confined to any one religion. It is rooted in experience and can include authenticity, letting go of the past, facing our fears, insight and forgiveness, love and compassion, community, awareness, peace and liberation. A cynic might say that this list has a New Age feel to it, perhaps reflecting Vaughan's Californian lifestyle. However, the vacuum left by the decline of conventional religion can be filled by a flight into consumerism as Cushman (1990) suggests or by a search for authentic spirituality. This existential quest for meaning, which may be seen as often masking the spiritual quest, is what perhaps leads many people to therapy.

COUNTERTRANSFERENCE MATTERS

It is imperative that we, as professionals, monitor our own resistances, countertransference issues, and value systems regarding spiritual and religious issues if we are to meet most ethically and efficaciously the special needs of our clients. (Lannert, 1991: 75)

One of the aims of therapist training including therapist personal development work is that trainees will become aware of their countertransference issues (or in person-centred terms, their difficulties with, or the subtleties of, being congruent). On many therapist training courses there is much focus on issues around gender, sexuality and ethnicity. This training does not eliminate all such countertransference, nor could it: indeed, countertransference reactions are often a valuable part of the therapeutic encounter. However, to become conscious of the part one's own material plays in such reactions is a crucial part of being an effective therapist.

Turning to religion and spirituality, it is of crucial importance that therapists in training and afterwards explore their views and attitudes. It is not sufficient to say, 'Well, I am an atheist' or 'My clients never raise any issues around spirituality'. Religion and spirituality are important to many people. As we have seen, a significant number of people do have spiritual experiences. Many such experiences are not problematic but some are, and Hay (1982) reports the taboo people had about disclosing such experiences. Allman's work also indicated how prejudiced therapists could be, either accepting all such mystical experiences as healthy or denying any health in such experiences. Clearly a number of her respondents were stuck in countertransference reactions. People's spirituality is more than just a question of having spiritual experiences (though these can occur within the therapy room as discussed in the previous chapter). Many people suffer from the consequences of a too harsh and rigid religious upbringing. During teenage years dilemmas and challenges to religious faith can arise where the therapist could be a safer figure to explore these matters than the priest, guru or rabbi. Bereavement is often a trigger for spiritual questioning, as is old age. A spiritually aware therapist can be open to such questioning arising and can invite the possibility by asking a simple question about the client's religious background during the initial assessment interview.

Spiritual Development of Therapists

Counsellor and psychotherapist training courses, with the possible exception of those on behavioural and cognitive approaches, usually involve some personal development work on the part of the trainee (McLeod, 1993). Indeed the British Association for Counselling from 1 October 1997 insisted that all new applicants for individual counsellor accreditation have at least 40 hours of personal development, which brought its members somewhat more in line with the demands for personal or training therapy on psychotherapy training courses. Psychotherapy training courses usually demand that their trainees receive personal therapy for the duration of their training. This can vary from one to three therapy sessions a week.

Various arguments have been advanced for this stance including that of equality: namely the importance of the therapist having experienced what it is like to be a client, and not asking a client to do something she or he has not themselves done or experienced. An equally, if not more powerful, argument put forward is that the wholeness, health and sensitivity of the therapist is increased by having their own therapy or analysis. This has yet to be backed up by research, and is indeed challenged by some research, but certainly many therapists will insist that this is so.

John Rowan (1989) takes this argument a stage further when he maintains that good psychotherapists should have their own spiritual discipline. Whilst I applaud this statement and feel that it is a prerequisite for effectively addressing spiritual issues within the therapy, it is arguably inappropriate to insist that all therapists follow a spiritual path. (Of course it could be suggested that life itself is a spiritual path.) Clearly some therapists deny the existence or the significance of spirituality and so could not in all honesty and integrity pursue a spiritual path, or some believe spirituality to be relevant but do not see themselves as being on a spiritual path. What I would call for is that all therapists during training are exposed to basic information about the major faiths within their society; various ways of mapping people's spiritual development; issues around spiritual emergence and awakening; a deep sense of their own relationship with religion and spirituality; and other topics explored in this and subsequent chapters.

However, models of therapist development tend to de-emphasize or even ignore the role of personal change, focusing primarily on the therapist's development as a practitioner. But the therapist is not a fixed, unchanging person who simply acquires therapeutic skills and then becomes increasingly effective in the practice of therapy. The process of personal change continues well beyond the end of the initial training, often subsumed under the heading of continuing professional development. Many therapists also comment on the impact of their work on their own development. This personal development of therapists can include the spiritual, which therefore needs to be considered as an aspect of therapist development.

A number of writers and researchers (Hawkins and Shohet, 1989; Skovholt and Ronnestad, 1992; Stoltenberg and Delworth, 1988) have explored and presented models of counsellor development, although these do not include the spiritual. So these models, whilst valuable as a key to understanding therapists' development, either do not go far enough, or are limited by their failure to include the spiritual in their view of human development and to allow for the possibility of the therapists working with spiritual issues. However, Dryden and Spurling edited a book *On Becoming a Psychotherapist* (1989) in which a number of contributors write about the role spirituality played in their lives.

Heron maintains that people who have done a lot of therapeutic work on their 'wounded child . . . tend to open up to transpersonal development' (1992: 83). Therapists open to their own development will tend to do likewise as a result of their own unfolding and also possibly triggered by their clients' explorations of these areas. Therapists often comment that their clients frequently work on issues that are currently alive in themselves.

It can also be argued, as discussed earlier, that the practice of being a therapist in which one pays attention to one's own inner processes whilst being simultaneously aware of one's client is in itself a spiritual practice akin to meditation (Tart and Deikman, 1991). Doing this week in, week out with clients over a period of years will inevitably lead to spiritual development in the therapist, some would say.

It is striking how a number of well known therapists, mostly male (Heron, 1992; Jung, 1967; Reich, 1969; Rogers, 1980; Rowan, 1993), began to take a deep interest in spirituality and the part it played in their work as they grew older. Of course such a phenomenon is not confined to therapists or to men. Maybe it represents a more striking change, a break with what Western men are raised to think and believe. For instance, Jocelyn Chaplin, talking of her early life, speaks of her rebellion against her family's Christianity: 'Yet I had some kind of inner strength, a faith in that harmony I had dreamt of as a child . . . I still had a sense of not being alone in a spiritual sense. It almost felt as though I had some kind of "inner" guide' (1989: 172). Looking back she feels that she would have liked someone who could 'connect with the spiritual as well as the emotional and sexual side of my life'. Years later she realizes that she wanted to be that therapist she never had.

RICHARD'S SPIRITUAL DEVELOPMENT

As a way of highlighting issues around the spiritual development of psychotherapists I shall include the story of Richard. During my doctoral study of therapy and healing I did a case study of Richard, one of the therapists I interviewed, who spoke at some length about his own spiritual development (for fuller details see West, 1995a: 338–47).

Richard is a Gestalt psychotherapist in his early 40s with more than 20 years' experience of counselling and groupwork. He lives in a northern British city where he works as a self-employed psychotherapist with individuals and groups. He also runs training groups and provides supervision.

Richard was born and brought up in a small, relatively isolated village in the Thames Valley. He had two sisters, both more than five years older than him. He felt quite alone as a child, taking himself off into the countryside, feeling somewhat separate or different from his peers, never quite being able to fit into the school gangs even though he wanted to. He developed a rich imaginative life, enjoying his own company, exploring the nearby river, woods and countryside.

As a child he was very sensitive to atmospheres. He believes he had to be since his family was very dysfunctional. His parents hated each other; their only real sign of contact was in fighting. Richard either got caught up between them or felt the emotional backlash from his mother. He learnt when a 'strike was in the air' or when something 'poisonous' was coming his way. He felt he 'absorbed stuff' from his mother to calm her down. He wanted to heal his parents and their relationship.

As a result of dealing with his parents and their conflicts he became very intuitive, something which he now uses in his work as a psychotherapist. His father had a psychotic breakdown when Richard was an adolescent. He feels his mother was always borderline (that is someone who has extreme difficulties in forming relationships and who has been profoundly emotionally damaged by childhood experiences and who expresses high levels of dependency and rage: McLeod, 1993). As his father's health deteriorated and he became violent, his mother began long, drawn-out divorce proceedings. Richard's detachment, rich fantasy life, and time away from home out in the countryside was a way of dealing with this.

Another way of coping as an adolescent was to turn to drugs, beginning with glue-sniffing and progressing to a variety of other substances. His drug-taking included psychedelics, which opened up his thinking about consciousness and spirituality. His interest in these areas was evident earlier in his life, for as a boy he had taken himself off to the local Anglican church, which was very much part of village life, though his parents did not attend or show any interest in religion. He finally pulled himself out of the drug culture at the age of 20, when his friends began increasingly to take heroin and cocaine.

Since the end of the 1980s Richard has begun to explore what spirituality means to him, as have many of his friends and peers. He has noticed a move among Gestalt psychotherapists to include spirituality in their holistic view of people. Richard's own spiritual exploration includes the creation-centred spirituality approach of Matthew Fox (1993), an ex-Benedictine monk who preaches about original blessing rather than emphasizing original sin.

Richard recognizes the impact of his own private spiritual exploration on his therapy work:

> On the one hand I think it enables me to facilitate people when they're working on spirituality issues themselves, and I think also it helps me when clients are in a less healthy type of mode. A lot of my clients are connected with the Church and have been brought up in a Christian way, [and] tend to have a restricted or even depressed mode of feeling, and my spirituality helps me to know that there's more than that. There is a tendency in the Church to force-feed people, to make them introject beliefs, whereas I think the thrust of Gestalt therapy is that we, rather than swallow things whole, we chew them over and spit out the bad bits, and swallow the good bits.

Soon after attending a five-day workshop on spirituality, and immediately following a supervision group which explored the issue of clients seeing ghosts and how to handle them in therapy, Richard had a significant spiritual experience which involved the presence of his then partner's dead father. A year later a non-human presence visited Richard, an experience that he felt to be a religious one:

> I was in a sort of meditative state somehow, and I started to get this sense of optimism inside, and started to feel very warm and strong and secure inside, which grew and grew and grew. And that point was when I became aware of an external presence in the archway, strangely, a very strong, sort of reassuring presence. And my feelings continued to grow stronger, and that's the point when I started to engage in a sort of dialogue with this phenomenon. It was an extremely high, emotionally charged experience for me. And I had some dialogue with this presence about my own sufferings and then about the sufferings of other people in the world, and there was the kind of answer that at the ultimate level everything was okay.

This description of Richard's fits the classic descriptions of spiritual or religious experiences (Hay, 1982) and their consequences. These in Richard's case were that 'it increased my courage and strength. And it helped me to be stronger with clients, and to encourage them to be courageous and to trust the universe really and trust life, which seems to work.'

Subsequently, Richard has experienced presences in his therapy room when he has been working with clients:

> On some occasions, particularly when working with bereavement, I've noticed that an almost tangible third presence sometimes comes into the room, maybe the spirit, the mark of the lost person. That's happened on a few occasions, and occasionally a presence can be felt that isn't human, that is maybe more divine, spiritual sort of thing.

If Richard felt that it was the person the client had lost

> I would consider that an ideal time to invite the client to talk to such a person. Usually they would engage in a very contactful kind of dialogue. Occasionally the client decides that they are not ready, but normally it's a good sign that it's a good time for dialogue with the lost person. Occasionally, it's God or a divine sort of presence that turns up. I often invite people to dialogue with God.

Such experiences would not only be troubling for many therapists, but would also raise issues in supervision. However, Richard's supervisor is also a priest and consequently comfortable with such experiences. He was able to help Richard look at it from a psychological perspective as well as from a spiritual or religious viewpoint. Richard commented: 'I think he was very useful in discouraging me from spending too much energy on trying to define the phenomenon.'

There are a number of noteworthy features that emerge from Richard's story that are worth commenting on:

1 Richard felt alone and set apart from others in his childhood, which is not uncommon for future psychotherapists (Dryden and Spurling, 1989) and healers (Courtenay, 1991).
2 Richard developed a high degree of sensitivity to other people and to atmospheres in order to cope with the dysfunctional family into which he was born. This not only contributed to his becoming a therapist but also enabled him to open to atmospheres and hence presences.
3 Richard demonstrated an interest in spiritual matters as a child, taking himself off to church on his own.
4 Richard has explored his spirituality as an adult through creation-centred spirituality and had been on a five-day workshop immediately prior to his first significant spiritual experience.
5 Richard has had striking spiritual experiences, both on his own and in therapy sessions, when he has been aware of the presence of people who have died, and of a divine presence.
6 These experiences have led Richard to think about how he could integrate his spirituality and his therapy work, through supervision and through his involvement in my research and the PsychoSpiritual Initiative.
7 Richard belongs to a Gestalt school which seems open to the possibility of spiritual phenomena and accepts that these may need to be worked through in psychotherapy. Richard also has some supportive colleagues.
8 Richard is fortunate in having a supervisor whose own spirituality is well developed and who is able to guide him in working with presences in therapy.

Richard's story is only one particular story that can be told but it does illustrate clearly how spiritual experiences and the spiritual development of a psychotherapist impact on his work.

MAPPING THE PSYCHOSPIRITUAL

Counselling and psychotherapy theories usually include models of human development. Indeed, the practice of therapy can be seen to be about helping people to mature, whether this is understood in terms of Freud's (1933) stages of ego development (oral, anal, phallic etc.), Erikson's (1977) eight stages of man, Jung's (1933) concept of individuation, Rogers's (1980) fully functioning individual or Maslow's (1970) self-actualization. However, such theories, with the exception of Jung's and those of transpersonal psychology, tend to ignore people's spiritual nature and development.

On the other hand, Wilber (1975; 1979b; 1980) with his spectrum of consciousness, Heron (1992; 1998) with his unique view of the transpersonal self, Chaplin (1989) with her spiral model, and Fowler (1981) with his stages of faith, all put forward models of human development that do include the spiritual. Benner (1988) suggests we have a choice: either we can view the psychological as separate from the spiritual, in which case we can comfortably say 'Yes, I as a therapist deal with the psychological, if it is a problem of religion or spirituality you can see a priest, guru, rabbi or whatever'; or we can see how interwoven the psychological and the spiritual are and how often they cannot be separated and thereby address the whole of it as a psychospiritual unity. Benner (1988) offers us a model that has two dimensions, a structural or psychological one, and a directional or spiritual one, whilst insisting on what he calls our 'psychospiritual unity'. Another perspective would be to view the psychological and the spiritual as constructs placed on the flow of varying experiences.

If Wilber and Heron are broadly correct that our mature development as human beings includes the spiritual realms, then it is to be expected that some clients in therapy will tend towards these realms, if not inhibited by their therapists. Heron (1992) maintains as mentioned earlier that people who have done a lot of therapeutic work on their 'wounded child' will tend to open up to the transpersonal. In my view therapists open to their own development will tend to do likewise, both as a result of their own unfolding and also possibly triggered by their clients' exploring of these areas. Awareness of the spiritual could therefore be seen as a later stage of therapist development.

If we accept this view that therapists can both open up more to the spiritual realms and find the same occurring in their clients, a question remains: is this rightfully a new stage of therapist development or does it signify a new category of helper? It certainly seems to require a change in thinking and a shift in therapist technique, well illustrated by Rogers's concept of presence quoted in Chapter 2, in which he mentions altered states, and acting in ways that he could not logically justify.

Turning to Ken Wilber, he presents his model in a number of books and articles (Wilber, 1975; 1979a; 1979b; 1980; 1983; 1990), and Rowan (1993) devotes two chapters of his book on the transpersonal to Wilber's model and its implications for therapists. Wilber has not been without his critics (e.g. Heron, 1992; 1998; Washburn, 1990) and supporters (e.g. Rowan, 1993; Vaughan, 1986; Walsh and Vaughan, 1994). Indeed he has been described as 'the Einstein of the transpersonal'. Consequently any consideration of spirituality and therapy which also includes the transpersonal has to take in Wilber.

Wilber's model is a spiritual one which neatly brings together insights from Western psychology and psychotherapy with those from Eastern forms of spiritual development. It is a model which includes 10 developmental stages with the tasks of each stage needing to be completed before the person can move onto the next stage. Each stage contains the preceding stages, rather like a Russian doll. The 10 stages are: pleroma, dual unity, body ego, membership self, mental ego, centaur, lower subtle, higher subtle, lower causal, higher causal. There is a final all inclusive or ultimate state of being, which Wilber refers to as Atman.

Wilber indicates the developmental tasks necessary at each stage and discusses the most useful forms of personal growth that would help resolve these tasks. This is where Wilber is perhaps at his most controversial. His message is that conventional secular Western therapies help us move effectively through the early stages to the centaur stage of body/mind integration, at which point Eastern forms of personal development prove more effective. To become a fully developed person Wilber would recommend psychotherapy followed by meditation.

Aspects of Wilber's model clearly show Eastern influences. For instance in a paper contrasting the Western psychotherapist with the Hindu guru, Vigne (1991) points out how the guru usually works with those of a sound mind who already practise regular meditation. According to Vigne the Western psychotherapist specializes in helping their clients adjust to normal life; the guru is there to help his clients develop spiritually.

Further illumination of this issue can be offered by John Rowan (1993) who put forward a modified model of Ken Wilber's spectrum of consciousness. Rowan reduces Wilber's 10-stage model to four stages: I have extracted some aspects of Rowan's model in a very reduced form as shown in Table 6.1. If we first focus on the row entitled 'traditional role of helper' we can see that for work with the mental ego the helper is seen by Rowan as an analyst offering psychoanalysis, cognitive-behavioural work or transactional analysis. If we then work with the real self we have the helper as growth facilitator, typically covered by humanistic approaches. However working with the soul requires the helper as advanced guide, offering a Jungian or transpersonal approach. If we wish to work at the level of spirit then the helper is outside the usually therapeutic mode and is a priest or priestess or sage.

So in Rowan's controversial frame, albeit derived from Wilber, the therapists at best can only work up to the level of soul, leaving work in the realms of the spirit to the sage or priest(ess). However, it may be that a therapist could move between these positions or roles as appropriate

Table 6.1   *Four positions in personal development (Rowan, 1993)*

Wilber level Rowan position	Persona/shadow Mental ego	Centaur Real self	Subtle self Soul	Causal self Spirit
Social goal	Socialization	Liberation	Extending	Salvation
Traditional role of helper	Physician or analyst	Growth facilitator	Advanced guide	Priest(ess), sage
Therapeutic approach	Psychoanalysis; cognitive-behavioural; some transactional analysis	T-groups Gestalt; open encounter; person-centred; bodywork	Psychosynthesis; some Jungian; transpersonal	Zen; Taoism; Christian mysticism; Sufi; some Judaism; Goddess; mystics

for their clients; there may not be such a rigid or linear differentiation between positions.

Heron (1998) offers a masterly critique of models of spiritual transcendence offered by Wilber, Grof and Wasburn, before presenting his own. Indeed he warns us not to place too much emphasis on maps: 'There is, in my view, no ultimate framework, only a range of provisional models, grounded in each author's developing experiential inquiry in what there is' (1998: 73).

Heron (1998) warns us against 'the lure of the East', of uncritical acceptance of models based on ancient Hindu and Buddhist mysticism without realizing their ancient and restrictive cultural context. Washburn is welcomed by Heron for his two-pole model of the ego and the ground, but is criticized for not including in his model an element for above, for the sky, that is both immanent and transcendent spirituality.

Washburn (1990) suggests that there are at least two separate models or patterns of spiritual development or transcendence: that of Wilber's which draws from Eastern spirituality and proposes a 'ladder to oneness', and the more Western view of a 'spiral to integration'. This 'spiral to integration' view draws on the work of Carl Jung and is based on the notion that in the first half of one's life one develops the ego. In the second half of life the inward journey is emphasized more, one returns to the beginning and knows it for the first time.

Washburn was prompted to write in favour of the Jungian viewpoint owing to the wide acceptance of Wilber's model in humanistic and transpersonal circles, especially in the USA. There has been some limited empirical research based on a small sample of Indian and English elderly in the USA which offers support for Wilber's model (Thomas and Brewer, 1993). Wilber (1990) wrote in reply to Washburn and suggested that the two models are not incompatible and that the Jungian model can be incorporated into his model.

Heron thinks that there has been an unthinking acceptance of Wilber's model, that we have lacked 'a proper degree of critical discrimination'

(1998: 76). Heron finds that Wilber's model does not relate to his experience in the following ways:

1 It shows no grasp of dynamic dipolarity of inwardness, i.e. the inner spiritual path is seen as being all about 'ascent' rather than 'descent'. Mary Swale (personal communication, 1999) senses it as 'going in' and 'going out' at the same time, that is an inner centring coupled with a sense of expanded consciousness.
2 The focus on ascent is related to the use of traditional oriental practices such as sitting meditation as a means of spiritual transformation in which the person is alone and immobile. Heron contrasts this with a more charismatic form of spiritual exploration which might use dance, voice and movement, such as that of the Sufis.
3 Heron argues that Wilber's model of proceeding in a more or less orderly way through lower stages to higher ones does not match his own experience, or that of other writers. I think Wilber's model or how it is presented could be adjusted to include this criticism.
4 Heron argues that we can have a working relationship with higher beings on the high subtle level, while for Wilber this is yet another stage to pass through on the way to Atman, the ultimate level.
5 There are problems with Wilber's view that any form of self is temporary, to be discarded as we progress to the next stage. Heron firmly proposes a model that includes horizontal as well as vertical ascent and descent and regards Wilber's model as losing so much and resulting in spiritual inflation with its focus on the Atman or final stage of human–divine development.
6 In Wilber's model we are returning to the one from which we are created, moving back up the stages already laid out. Heron sees this as a conservative and uncreative view of spiritual development. Many would share the poet Wordsworth's view of the spirituality of children and the potential for soul development in the child as discussed by Hillman (Moore, 1990).

Indeed at its worst Wilber's model can be seen as overly rigid and hierarchical. Heron (1998) is also critical of transpersonal psychology for being dominated by male therapists who advocate experiential spiritual training within a traditional, usually Buddhist, school. Heron insists that what he seeks is a dialogue based on individual experience. He most certainly does not want to be told what developmental stage he is at within some map created elsewhere. I can sympathize with his viewpoint but I also value the creation of maps where they can help us. Wilber's map as interpreted by Rowan and simplified in my table does help us relate client problems to possibly better therapeutic solutions.

I have included the debate about Wilber's model in some detail as well as presenting something of Jung's and Heron's models. Which model we choose can have a huge impact on how we work with our clients, including the choosing of no apparent model at all. Perhaps we can be guided by considering the consequences of the spiritual position taken by our clients or better still we can attempt to work with our clients' models whilst remembering that the 'map is not the territory'.

As a final comment on maps the agonized comments of one member of the PsychoSpiritual Initiative are relevant: 'Every time I go to supervision and they bring in a map. They say next time you want to do this. I do it and it screws up a session completely.' Maps are there to benefit ourselves and our clients; when they cease so to do then we must discard them.

PHENOMENOLOGY

'Laws as such do not make people better,' said Nasrudin to the king; 'they must practise certain things, in order to become attuned to inner truth. This form of truth resembles apparent truth only slightly.'

The King decided that he could, and would, make people observe the truth. He could make them practise truthfulness. His city was entered by a bridge. On this he built a gallows. The following day, when the gates were opened at dawn, the captain of the Guard was stationed with a squad of troops to examine all who entered. An announcement was made: 'Everyone will be questioned. If he tells the truth, he will be allowed to enter. If he lies, he will be hanged.'

Nasrudin stepped forward.

'Where are you going?'

'I am on my way,' said Nasrudin slowly, 'to be hanged.'

'We don't believe you!'

'Very well, if I have told a lie, hang me!'

'But if we hang you for lying, we will have made what you said come true!'

'That's right: now you know what truth is – YOUR truth!' (from Idries Shah, 1969)

If spirituality is to fully play its part in the therapeutic encounter then there needs to be some perspective from which the therapist can view and understand the part it plays. In Chapter 2 I considered the main therapeutic approaches and explored the difficulties inherent within each in terms of working with clients' (and their therapists') spirituality.

The therapist will undoubtedly have her or his own views on spirituality. What I am concerned with here is how the therapist can be present to their clients' own experiencing of spirituality within their lives and within the therapy room. This question of what perspective to take is not solved by the therapist taking a particular religious stance. (This can of course be a good solution for working with members of one's own religious faith which can then bring the therapist close to being a spiritual director.) A flexible therapist working within a religious frame may well be able to be supportive of a client's spiritual explorings and musings. However, there will often be sticking points, however flexible the religious therapist is. For example, consider a Christian therapist faced with the following dilemmas raised by their client:

1 Client becoming involved in pagan or Goddess worship.
2 Client developing an interest in astrology and the occult.
3 Client becoming a fundamentalist and joining a cult.
4 Client seeking an abortion.
5 Client claiming to have experienced past lives.
6 Client seeking a spiritual healer.
7 Client experiencing dead relatives as present within the therapy room.

All of these are phenomena that have arisen within my own therapeutic practice. Any or all of these phenomena may present difficulties to a very religiously based Christian therapist. One can imagine equivalent difficulties for Buddhist, Hindu, Jewish, Islamic and other religiously based therapists.

A possible way forward is offered by the philosophical approach known as phenomenology. I will not attempt a detailed discussion and description of phenomenology here, but briefly phenomenology is a school of philosophy developed by Husserl which 'takes the view that valid knowledge and understanding can be gained by exploring and describing the ways things are experienced by people' (McLeod, 1993: 67). The basic idea of a phenomenological approach rests on our inner experiencing and it insists on 'the crucial value of returning to the self to discover the nature and meaning of things as they appear and in their essence' (Moustakas, 1994: 26).

To approach people as either researcher or therapist using phenomenology involves bracketing off our assumptions about them and the phenomena they are experiencing. Phenomenology deals with our experiences of reality, not with reality itself. Consequently within a phenomenological framework I cannot say that your experience is wrong or unreal. I can say it is uncommon or that to have such a view of reality will lead to disturbing consequences. So a phenomenological viewpoint deeply respects the reality of the other person. The challenge for the therapist is to follow the client in their exploring of their reality. Inevitably the therapist's own world view impacts on the client, but the more the therapist can bracket this the better. Heron (1992) reminds us that total bracketing is not possible. However, to attempt it is important.

It will be apparent that phenomenological ideas have their place in modern therapy. They have especially influenced humanistic approaches in general and Gestalt, person-centred and existentialist therapies among others in particular.

To use a phenomenological approach has its limitations. Firstly, as has already been mentioned, complete bracketing is impossible, so it is important to remember that we filter knowledge in various ways, and thus a phenomenological approach is not a solution to this dilemma. Secondly, although we will inevitably attempt to get alongside our clients, a phenomenological way of viewing people is itself a way of structuring reality, has its own set of values and ethics which may well be different from that of our client's. Our client may wish us to be within their religious frame, or to be a detached objective professional, or a secular observer, and so on. It is quite possible that our client will want several differing, perhaps contradictory perspectives from us, some of which they may well be unconscious of. Indeed some clients will probably be frustrated by a phenomenological approach and want us to come down on one side or the other in relation to, for example, spiritual phenomena, rather than have us put the ball therapeutically back into their court by saying, 'What do you think?'

EXISTENTIALISM

> Existential psychotherapy is a dynamic approach to therapy which focuses on concerns that are rooted in the individual's existence. (Yalom, 1980: 5)

> Existentialism is a philosophy which aims to understand or illuminate the experience of 'being-in-the-world'. The focus is therefore on the way of being of the person, the qualitative texture of his or her relationship with self (*Eigenwelt*), others (*Mitwelt*) and the physical world (*Umwelt*). (McLeod, 1998: 190)

Closely related to phenomenology is existentialism; indeed some link them together and refer to phenomenological existentialism. As well as being a key influence on many forms of humanistic therapy, existentialism has also led to schools of existential therapy in the USA, Britain and elsewhere in Europe. Existential therapists believe that we have a 'thrown condition'. We are made, we appear from eternity, have a brief life and return to eternity. Therapeutic progress is possible if clients are willing to confront the givens of their existence. Yalom (1980) suggests that these givens are death, freedom, meaninglessness and isolation. Underneath the neurotic anxiety presented by clients in therapy is seen to be an existential anxiety. Yalom insists that unlike Freudian analysis the basic conflict in existential therapy is 'a conflict that flows from the individual's confrontation with the givens of existence' (1980: 8).

Frankl (1947; 1973; 1978) was a psychoanalyst and an existentialist who called his approach to therapy Logotherapy. He was imprisoned by the Nazis for three years in Auschwitz and Dachau where he found that 'Only those who were orientated towards the future, towards a goal in the future, towards a meaning to fulfil in the future, were likely to survive' (Frankl, 1978: 135). Frankl argued that there was an existential vacuum at the heart of twentieth-century life that could only be filled by God: 'As to the feeling of meaninglessness *per se*, it is an existential despair and a spiritual distress rather than an emotional disease or a mental illness' (1978: 134).

Frankl believed that a religious sense was present in everyone, perhaps buried in the unconscious. He regarded religion as a human phenomenon which he saw as 'an outgrowth of what I regard to be the most human of all human phenomena, namely the "will to meaning". Religion, we may say, revealed itself as the fulfilment of what we now may call the "will to ultimate meaning"' (1978: 153).

Existentialism and existential therapy focus on the struggle by the individual to give meaning to her or his life. Such an approach would support an individual client in exploring what spirituality or religion meant to them personally, if anything.

It would be inappropriate to complete a consideration of existentialism in relationship to spirituality without mentioning the life and work of Paul Tillich (1886–1965). Tillich in his ground breaking book *The Courage To Be* speaks of the importance of the courage to be, 'which is based on mystical union with the ground of being as well as in our description of the courage to be which is based on the personal encounter with God' (1952: 163). To Tillich the courage to be is an expression of faith, and such faith is not an opinion but a state of being. He advocates the acceptance of doubt and meaninglessness, indeed the inclusion of not-being with being, and points to Jesus Christ on the cross expressing his own doubt. He concludes: 'The courage to be is rooted in the God who appears when God has disappeared in the anxiety of doubt' (1952: 180).

We have already briefly considered the concept of the I–Thou and the I–It relationships developed by the existentialist philosopher Martin Buber which have had a big impact on therapy (Feltham, 1995). Buber's I–Thou relationship is concerned with the mystery of existence itself, with *being*; and, as Colin Purcell-Lee insists, 'One cannot approach the I–Thou relationship as a spectator or objective thinker' (1999: 11). Consequently it is not possible to empirically investigate Buber's I–Thou relationship. Nevertheless his poetic description of the I–Thou relationship strikes a chord with many people and it is hardly surprising to find claims made, however misguided, that people experience such relationships.

An acceptance of the possibility of I–Thou relating seems to provide an answer to existential meaninglessness. For Buber (1970) there were three spheres in which the world of relation, of I–Thou, arises: with nature, with persons, and with spiritual beings or what he called 'intellectual essences' like art, poetry and knowledge. There is a sense of deep spirituality in Buber's writings about I–Thou that seems to place it within the same existential spiritual territory as Frankl's Logotherapy.

Of course phenomenology, existentialism or phenomenological existentialism are all ideas that arose in Western culture. Indeed existentialism has been criticized for focusing too exclusively on the individual and his or her solutions to the dilemmas, and thereby downplaying the role of family and community and the part they play in the client's problem and its possible solution. However postmodern we become (and postmodern ideas are themselves a product of global capitalist culture) we cannot step outside culture and examine it free of any bias.

Having explored the background and underlying issues of meeting the challenge of how therapists can be present to their clients' spirituality, we now turn to the more specific questions of what techniques to use and how to integrate them into effective therapeutic work with clients.

7

Meeting the Challenge: Practice

In this chapter the focus shifts from considering the issues around spirituality in the background to the therapeutic encounter to a more direct exploration of the part spirituality can play in the therapy session, including the kind of spiritual interventions possible, contraindications for their use, supervision issues and some case examples.

SPIRITUAL INTERVENTIONS

In a recent book published by the American Psychological Association, Richards and Bergin (1997) argue the case for a spiritual strategy for counselling and psychotherapy. They put forward and discuss in some detail a by no means exhaustive list of possible interventions. These include:

> Praying for clients, encouraging clients to pray, discussing theological concepts, making references to scriptures, using spiritual relaxation and imagery techniques, encouraging forgiveness, helping clients live congruently with their spiritual values, self-disclosing spiritual beliefs or experiences, consulting with religious leaders, and using religious bibliotherapy. (1997: 128)

They emphasize that great care should be taken before using any such interventions and indicate that some of the above approaches can only be made by spiritually minded therapists. Contraindications for spiritual interventions are explored and discussed below. Richards and Bergin (1997) point to the extensive research evidence which backs up to some extent many of these interventions.

Richards and Bergin (1997) are writing within an American and theistic framework. Nevertheless it should prove valuable to examine their categories and consider how applicable they are to the British context. What is also of note as previously discussed is that spiritual interventions are being used by many if not all of the main schools of therapy.

Prayer

> Whatever prayer may mean to a counsellor, it may mean many other things to the client. (Rose, 1996: 8)

Table 7.1 *Prayer behaviours in order of frequency, from in-depth interviews with counsellors (Rose, 1993)*

Behaviour	Frequency ($n = 11$)
Pray when feeling anxious	9
Ask for help for self as counsellor	8
Contemplation/meditation on client/problem	7
Pray privately in session	6
Name clients in prayer	6
Pray for all clients routinely	5
Discuss prayer with clients (client's instigation)	5
Pray before sessions	5
Pray for clients during communal worship	5
Set aside time to pray for clients	4
Use prayer interactively with supervision	4
Pray at odd times (e.g. while driving car)	4
Refuse to pray overtly in session	4
Pray only for some clients	3
Pray overtly in session	3
Discuss prayer (therapist's instigation)	3
Go to a specific place to pray for clients	3
Pray for specific help for client	3
Allow thoughts about clients to emerge in wordless prayer	3
Pray for work as therapist	3
Discuss God (client's instigation)	2
Pray at prearranged time with client at time of separation	2
Third person prays silently in room throughout session	1

Prayer, as Rose (1996) remarks, is not generally spoken about in therapist training courses or among colleagues. However, she insists that even if it is not discussed in psychological circles, that does not mean it is not going on. Indeed we do know that some therapists do pray for their clients in the USA, Britain and elsewhere. For example in my own study of 19 British therapists who were also Quakers I found that 14 did pray on occasion for their clients (West, 1998a). In a detailed qualitative study of 11 therapists who all prayed for their clients, Rose (1993) found that six of her respondents prayed privately in sessions, three prayed overtly in sessions, although four sometimes refused to pray overtly, and six named clients in prayer.

Rose's (1993) research shows that the use of prayer in therapy is not simply a matter of prayer by the therapist for the client within or outside the session (see Table 7.1). Prayer may be used by the therapist to help their work with their client or to focus on their client and their problem, perhaps when the therapy work feels stuck.

Rose speaks of the reluctance of clients to raise the question of prayer, and drawing on her own experience she states: 'I myself have often found that trying to talk about prayer on a personal level can be as risky and potentially shameful as talking about sex, and is treated with equal caution within church communities' (1996: 9). She draws our attention to the value of prayer by clients between sessions for those clients who do habitually pray: 'Prayer can be a place where, between sessions, they process some of the deep psychological pain they are going through' (1996: 9).

The respondents in Rose's research saw the positive use of prayer as a resource, as a form of nourishment, and as a way of channelling or accessing power or healing. Of course the use of prayer by clients can serve as a defence against change, against taking responsibility for their own lives; so the role of prayer in the life of the client and the therapist and in the therapeutic relationship needs careful monitoring and supervision.

There are a number of ethical and other issues that need to be considered here. Is it ethical to pray for someone, especially a client, without their consent? Many clients would no doubt welcome the idea of their therapist praying for them, but even so it will have an impact on the therapeutic alliance, for example it will probably affect the transference. Richards and Bergin point out that 'Praying with clients during sessions increases the risk that role boundaries will become confused' (1997: 204).

There is however a further ethical problem that needs addressing. We have some evidence, albeit limited but statistically significant (Byrd, 1988; Richards and Bergin, 1997), that prayer may impact positively on its recipients' health. Knowing that prayer is possibly beneficial, are we justified in refusing it?

Rose (1996) raises the question of whether praying for clients is ethical within the BAC Code of Ethics and Practice for Counsellors (1996), and she concludes that if such actions form part of 'working in ways which promote the client's control over his/her own life' then prayer is ethical. However, if prayer is some kind of action on behalf of clients then she feels it is not ethical.

Encouraging clients to pray seems to take the therapeutic relationship and turn it into something akin to spiritual direction. Nevertheless with religiously inclined clients this might just be appropriate. It could well fit into the increasingly popular notion of giving clients some kind of 'homework' to do. Such an approach is often welcomed by clients.

Bruce Liese (1998) describes a dramatic cure by prayer of his own fear of flying which arose following a traumatic incident in which a plane he was travelling in fell over 1000 feet. Liese applied all his knowledge of cognitive behaviourism to overcome his phobia and nothing worked. One day, once more on a plane and once more suffering symptoms of panic and fearing for his life, he decided, being Jewish, to pray. His prayer was the Kaddish which is the Jewish prayer for the dead. Immediately his symptoms disappeared, never, as yet, to return.

Discussing Theological Concepts and Making References to Scriptures

Richards and Bergin (1997) among others suggest that during assessment sessions with would-be clients it is valuable to ask the clients about their religious and spiritual background and beliefs. Among other consequences of such an action is that it will signal to the client that exploring their spirituality as part of their therapy is welcome, should they so choose. In assessing the significance of their religious faith, or lack of it, the therapist is then able to judge whether reference to scriptures is or is not a potentially useful part of the client's therapy. It enables the therapist to operate more clearly within the client's frame of reference. For example within the case study of the Buddhist man discussed later in this chapter, the therapist at one point posed the question of whether his harsh view of himself fitted in with the Buddhist teachings. This proved to be an effective challenge.

Discussing theological concepts feels appropriate only if raised by the client in a context in which the therapist is clear about his or her limitations as a theologian. If client and therapist happen to share the same denominational background such discussion can prove valuable to the client. It is important that therapists working with religiously minded clients have some knowledge of their religions so that they can be as effective as possible.

Using Spiritual Relaxation and Imagery Techniques

The use of relaxation and imagery is a valuable component of the skills base of the practising integrative or eclectic therapist. Such powerful techniques need to be used appropriately after adequate assessment that the client would benefit and appropriate training for the therapist in using such techniques. A therapist possessing competence in these techniques should be able quite easily to introduce spiritual imagery.

There is evidence of the effectiveness of such therapeutic work. For example Propst et al. (1992) working in the USA found that, in treating 59 religious subjects suffering from depression, those offered cognitive-behavioural therapy using religious imagery or pastoral counselling with priests had lower depression and higher adjustment scores after 18–20 sessions than those offered standard cognitive-behavioural therapy or on a waiting list. The differences were less marked after three-month and two-year follow-ups. Two implications emerge from this study: (1) the therapist involved does not have to have a religious faith to work effectively with clients in this way; (2) the relative success of the pastoral counselling group suggests the benefits that might result from its greater use.

Encouraging Forgiveness

Forgiveness is a key component of pastoral care (Jeff, 1987; Leech, 1994; Lyall, 1995). Leech insists that 'confession and forgiveness lie at the heart of the Christian experience' (1994: 200). Although forgiveness has been explored as an element in psychotherapy, the models generated have had little impact on research and practice (McCullogh and Worthington, 1994). It could be argued that one of the key limitations of the largely secular practices of counselling and psychotherapy is their lack of the recognition of the key role of forgiveness in psychological healing. Indeed critics of secular therapists have questioned their tendency to encourage 'parent blaming' or 'partner blaming'.

Enright (1996) suggests that we examine forgiveness in three aspects: forgiving others, forgiving self and receiving forgiveness. Recent research has indicated that the frequency of use of forgiveness may correlate with the spiritual beliefs of the therapist involved (DiBlasio and Proctor, 1993). There is suspicion within the therapy world of encouraging premature forgiveness in cases where clients have not been sufficiently supported in working through any appropriate anger and other feelings involved. An overly Christian approach can focus too easily on premature search for forgiveness (McNeice, 1996). As Richards and Bergin point out: 'When people attempt to forgive prematurely, the healing process is prevented from occurring, and invalidated and unresolved feelings of pain, grief, guilt, shame, anger, and rage continue to create problems for them in their lives' (1997: 213).

Despite these caveats we find that encouraging forgiveness is one of the most frequently used spiritual interventions by psychotherapists (Richards and Bergin, 1997). In the end, for forgiveness to be effective and healing it needs to be carried out by the client in their own time, but even so sometimes the sense of hurt and damage is so great that forgiveness cannot be achieved.

Helping Clients Live Congruently with their Religious Values

Therapy, despite what some practitioners would like to think, is not a value-free process. This is not to say that therapists should impose their values on their clients. Nevertheless it is important for therapists to be clear with themselves and where appropriate their clients as to what values underpin their work.

Richards and Bergin (1997) argue that a client who acts in contradiction to his or her value system will suffer emotional and interpersonal distress. They advocate helping the client to become aware of such inconsistencies including whether their religious and spiritual beliefs give rise to guilt and anxiety or comfort and strength. They suggest that in cases of value–lifestyle incongruence it may well be useful for the therapist to help clients identify and own such incongruencies. For example all Islamic and some Christian groups prohibit the use of alcohol. Any client belonging to such a group and drinking on a regular basis has an incongruence which may well give rise to inner tensions. Religious groups of many denominations take moral stances around sexuality and marriage which again give rise to tensions between the person and their faith.

Self-Disclosing Spiritual Beliefs or Experiences

Self-disclosure by the therapist in order to help the client is an accepted practice if used appropriately, within the humanistic schools of therapy.

Rowan (1976) refers us to the work of Jourard among others on the value of self-disclosure by the therapist as a way of encouraging the same in the client. One aspect of Rogers's (1951) core conditions, namely congruence, can involve self-disclosure on the part of the therapist. The intuitive timing and knowing if and when to disclose can impact very beneficially on the client. It is in this territory that we perhaps may reach Rogers's 'presence' (Kirschenbaum and Henderson, 1990a) or Buber's (1970) I–Thou, discussed in Chapter 2.

However, going beyond simpler forms of self-disclosure to sharing of one's own spiritual beliefs and experiences feels much more risky for the whole project of therapy. Such disclosure needs to be offered within the context of a very trusting therapeutic alliance. Indeed, the challenge therapists face in such self-disclosure is in not overwhelming the client with the material or structuring the client's experience within their own frame. Such disclosures need to be offered very tentatively and in a way that enables the client to pick them up or reject them as appropriate.

Consulting with Religious Leaders

In the USA there is probably a greater culture among health care professionals of team management of the therapy and treatment of clients and patients. However, it is increasingly the case in Britain that therapists may well be involved (with clients' permission of course) in liaison with general practitioners and other health professionals. The notion of being in contact with a client's religious leader is rather a novel one, but once the concept of collaboration or liaison with other professionals who can benefit the client is accepted, maybe it is not such a strange idea. Such an approach is probably likely to remain limited whilst the therapy world in Britain remains hostile to organized religion. The other factor to acknowledge is that attendance at conventional religious services remains much higher in the USA than in Britain, and therefore the use of religious leaders in this way is more possible.

Using Religious Bibliotherapy

According to Richards and Bergin (1997) the use of scriptures and sacred writings is the most frequent spiritual intervention undertaken by therapists, even though little research has been conducted into their use as a separate intervention. They counsel therapists drawn to using such writings to only use those that are compatible with their clients' spiritual beliefs. Such approaches include: therapists quoting sacred writings to clients; interpreting such writings to clients; making indirect references to such writings while disclosing or teaching religious concepts; relating stories from sacred writings; encouraging clients to read and study such texts outside sessions; using sacred writings to challenge clients' dysfunctional and irrational beliefs.

It will be apparent from this list how potentially powerful such an approach will be with a client who regards themselves as spiritual. However, by their very power the use of sacred writings needs to be done with great care and the therapist will need to bear in mind that they are not the client's religious teacher, and that the use of the sacred writings is to further the client's therapeutic progress. In recent times there has been an increased popularity in self-help and New Age books, and the Christian psychiatrist M. Scott Peck (1990) has written extensively about Christian values and spiritual growth.

In addition to the spiritual interventions offered by Richards and Bergin (1997) and discussed so far, there are two further potentially valuable spiritual interventions: asking religious questions during assessment interviews, and the use of intuition/inspiration.

Asking Religious Questions During Assessment

We have already examined the use of assessment procedures that include the client's spirituality in the previous chapter. Many therapists advocate routinely asking clients about their religious background including any spiritual practices they might engage in (Richards and Bergin, 1997). By asking such questions the therapist indicates to the client the importance she or he attaches to religion and spirituality, thereby enabling the client to be more able to speak about such matters.

The question about spiritual practices is especially important in Britain where, despite a decline in church attendance, many people engage in various forms of spiritual expression including prayer, healing rituals, meditation and retreats. It will be apparent that to mention spirituality and religion during assessment in itself constitutes an intervention, whether we are merely undertaking a level 1 or level 2 assessment (see Figure 6.1) advocated by Richards and Bergin (1997) or some other form of assessment.

Use of Intuition/Inspiration

'Intuition' is defined (*Oxford English Dictionary*, 1989) as the immediate apprehension of an object by the mind, intellect or senses without the intervention of any reasoning process. It can be transpersonal according to Rowan (1993) and Clark (1979), and it is of note that Rogers at one time considered using it as one of his core conditions. Intuition has a range of meanings that can include both the mundane and the transcendent. As a result it can serve as a bridge into the spiritual and the transpersonal. However, it can also be used as a container, as a barrier in which spiritual insights can be dismissed as 'mere intuition', especially if they are seen to be emanating from a woman. Intuition was, however, one of Jung's (1933) four psychological functions of human beings, the others being thinking, feeling and sensing.

In my research into Quaker therapists (West, 1998a) mentioned previously, I asked those interviewed if they ever felt inspired during their work in a way similar to ministry in a Quaker meeting for worship. ('Ministry' used in this sense refers to how Quakers will speak when spiritually moved to, thus breaking the silence of a Quaker meeting.). Out of the 18 respondents, 13 replied 'sometimes' or 'frequently'. I suspect that this use of inspiration or 'ministry' within a therapy session is more common with these Quaker therapists than their secular colleagues. Some of their comments were:

I have a feeling in a session of sometimes being taken beyond just what I can do. It's a feeling almost of words coming out of my mouth that I didn't know were going to be spoken, that sense of almost being taken beyond my knowing which I sense is a bit like ministry.

There were almost tangible moments in my counselling where I was being talked through, it was rather like ministry . . . I suddenly seemed to speak very pointedly to my clients, and afterwards, when I heard the echo of myself spoken, I thought, 'Wow, did I say that?'

I can find myself making a suggestion about something or saying something to a client which I don't feel comes entirely from me.

I have quite a strong dependency on intuition, and presumably it's the same quality that informs ministry as informs empathic understanding of where a client might be.

There is a sense of something going on which is more than the interaction of the counsellor and the client at best . . . the point at which one suddenly gets an insight for no particular reason . . . that wasn't there before and seems to come from nowhere . . . an outside input to either counsellor or client.

I am struck by the fact that none of the respondents actually claims that their inspiration was ministry. Nevertheless the experience of actually ministering in a Quaker meeting for worship would I think make it easier and more likely for these therapists to surrender to a similar impulse in their therapy work.

Taking the therapeutic interventions of a spiritual nature discussed above, ranging from prayer through to bibliotherapy, they seem to represent a very powerful bundle of potentially therapeutic interventions. The transferential and other implications of such approaches need to be borne in mind especially within the supervision relationship which will be considered below.

Non-Interventions

However, there are other ways in which therapists impact on their clients besides intentional interventions. There are various elements that add up to the client possibly experiencing the therapy room as a 'spiritual space', which were explored in Chapter 5. Here I want to highlight two 'non-interventions': the therapist's own spiritual journey; and spiritual preparation by the therapist before and between sessions.

Therapist's Own Spiritual Journey

It is difficult, if not impossible, to quantify the impact of the therapist's own spiritual journeying on their clients. However, on the unconscious level it is very likely that the client will in some tacit way know or intuit that their therapist is spiritually awake, which should act to encourage the client to consider that part of their being. There seems a curious and unconscious alchemy or synchronicity (Jung, 1933) that brings a particular client to a particular therapist at a particular time, resulting often in a growthful experience for both involved.

The client's journey is a common metaphor within the person-centred and other humanistic schools of therapy (McLeod, 1993). The therapist regards himself or herself as a supporter, witness and fellow traveller who is alongside the client, occasionally slightly ahead or behind. From this perspective clients are seen as coming to therapy when the going gets tough and seeking help with the current stage of their journey through life rather than necessarily seeking a once and for all time in-depth cure.

For the spiritually minded client and/or therapist the client's journey will be regarded as a spiritual journey, as made clear by a number of the respondents in my researches with Quaker therapists:

> If I am with someone as a counsellor, there's a sense in which I see their struggle . . . as a spiritual journey in the widest sense.

> There is part of us that is creative and can lead to deeper integrity and deeper truth about ourselves, 'that of God in everyone' (a commonly used Quaker phrase that points to that of God within each of us), and that and the therapeutic journey are in my book identical. I can't make a distinction with the spiritual bit: the two in me merge.

Spiritual Preparation Before and Between Sessions

Many therapists talk of how they 'psych up' before a client arrives for a session, that is the kind of things they do to prepare themselves for the therapeutic encounter. Not surprisingly we find that many spiritually minded therapists engage in prayer, meditation, contemplation and other spiritual practices before and between seeing clients.

In Rose's (1993) research into the use of prayer by 11 therapists she found that five of them regularly prayed before a therapy session. In my research into Quaker therapists, respondents were asked if they spiritually prepared themselves in any way before seeing a client, for example by prayer, centring down, sitting in silence. I found that 15 (83 per cent) were engaged in some kind of spiritual preparation sometimes or frequently.

Even before a session, if I've got five minutes I may pray, particularly if it's one I know is going to be difficult. I will try and just centre . . . I let go of my own agenda and become connected with a much deeper reality and energy source.

I wouldn't draw up at somebody's house for example. I would stop my car somewhere away from the house and sit quietly. I wouldn't rush in all over the place . . . There's that peace and calmness now which I never had before . . . It's centring down, really, to be ready for what you are going to do.

'Centring down' is the name given to the process whereby those attending the Quaker meeting attempt to forget their daily lives and the outside world, and concentrate on the spiritual dimension of the silence (Dandelion, 1996).

Finally, having acknowledged the wide range of possible spiritual interventions, how should the spiritually inclined therapist go about using such approaches? Richards and Bergin (1997) advise against a cookbook approach. They suggest we carefully tailor our work with the client to fit their unique needs, beliefs and circumstances. The guiding principles behind such a way of working are:

1 a deep respect for the client's autonomy and freedom
2 sensitivity to and empathy for the client's religious and spiritual beliefs
3 flexibility and responsiveness to the clients' values and needs.

CONTRAINDICATIONS FOR SPIRITUAL INTERVENTIONS

Spiritual interventions, as discussed above, can have a powerful impact on the client (and on the therapist also). They need to be handled carefully and used appropriately under effective supervision. Richards and Bergin (1997) in their *Spiritual Strategy* book suggest that contraindictions for such work within the USA include: clients who do not want such an approach; clients who are delusional or psychotic; cases where spiritual issues are not relevant to the client's presenting problem; and where clients are minors and parental consent has not been obtained for such interventions.

Clearly such an approach will not be fruitful with someone who does not want it; likewise with someone who does not see the point of such an intervention with regard to their specific problem. For example people who view God as distant and condemning are unlikely to respond to the use of prayer; likewise those with a passive view who feel that there is little they can do as it is 'all in God's hands'.

Richards and Bergin (1997) warn us that therapist-initiated, denominationally specific, religiously explicit, and in-session spiritual interventions are probably more risky than client-initiated, ecumenical, religiously implicit, and out-of-session interventions. A good therapeutic alliance is necessary for such interventions. Low therapist–client agreement on religious values mitigates against spiritual interventions. The context in which the therapy occurs is important. Private practice, where perhaps no third party is involved, or religious settings, where a spiritual approach may well be welcome, are probably less risky than health service and other public settings for spiritual interventions, where there may be restrictions on the use of such interventions or where therapeutic work is regarded as secular.

Informed consent is clearly of crucial importance here. If the initial assessment of the client has involved questions about their religious background and spiritual practices then discussion of possible spiritual interventions will be easier to make. However, any indication by the client that they would not welcome such an approach must be respected. It is important that the client clearly consents to each such spiritual intervention and it may well be appropriate to obtain their written consent. Again careful supervision is a imperative.

Richards and Bergin's discussion of contraindications of spiritual interventions ends with this caveat on behalf of the therapist:

> Of course, spiritual interventions are less likely to be used effectively and ethically by therapists who lack multicultural and religious sensitivity and awareness, have limited denominational expertise, and are spiritually immature. (1997: 253)

SUPERVISION

Supervision, whether of an individual, a peer or a group nature, is mandatory for all schools of counsellors and many schools of psychotherapists in Britain. For many therapists supervision is experienced as the support of a more seasoned colleague, a safe setting within which difficulties arising from work can be explored with the aim of improving the effectiveness of the therapy for the client involved. However, supervision can have its downside and instances of supervision abuse have occurred (Kaberry, 1999). Even if the supervisory relationship is not of an abusive nature it can become stuck and ineffectual in its main aim of promoting the best possible treatment for the client involved.

Any therapist working with the kind of spiritual interventions discussed above, or having spiritual experiences in sessions, requires high quality supervision from a supervisor familiar with and competent to supervise on these spiritual issues. This is a tall order when we reflect on the lack of spiritual content within many or most therapist training courses (Swinton, 1996).

Not surprisingly these issues have shown up in research including my two studies relating to therapist spirituality (West, 1995a; 1995b; 1997; 1998a). The first study was into counsellors and psychotherapists whose work included healing. One of the key findings of this research was that eight of the 30 therapists interviewed reported experiences of supervision difficulties. Some of the comments made to me included:

> I'm very careful whom I talk to about it [spirituality], even my supervisor.

I am losing supervisors as they generally consider I am helping people to become schizoid.

I don't feel the client has been helped [by supervision], and I feel in some way there's some sacred thing that has happened that has been exposed to the [supervision] group, that has not affirmed the sacredness of what was going on in the counsellor/client relationship.

It is of course possible that the therapists who took part in this research in response to a letter of mine in various publications (*Self & Society, Counselling*) were more likely to be those who experienced some dilemmas and difficulties. Nevertheless my research points to some of the issues faced by therapists whose work with their clients involves healing and spirituality.

However, not everyone in the study had such supervision difficulties. One very experienced therapist solved his supervision needs by having a supervisor who was both a therapist and a former priest. This was especially helpful when, working with several clients, the therapist found himself addressing the issue of spirit presences in the therapy room:

Fortunately my supervisor is familiar with these phenomena because he is a priest, or was a priest, and so he's capable of looking at it from a psychological perspective . . . and looking at it from a spiritual, religious perspective. I think he was useful in discouraging me from spending too much energy on trying to define the phenomenon.

The second study, inspired by the first, was into the impact of counsellors' and psychotherapists' spiritual beliefs on their work, interviewing therapists who were also Quakers. In this study five of the 18 therapists interviewed reported supervision difficulties. Some of their comments are:

I found that when I did have one client for whom the spiritual was very important, it was quite difficult to deal with, being supervised by someone who had no sense of the spiritual . . . either I took what I'd done to supervision and got it rubbished or I left it outside supervision.

There are moments I think when you almost feel a presence . . . I feel most humbled by those experiences, it's almost like being present to something that's really beyond what you could do, there is a sense of at-one-ness . . . This would not be easy to share with my supervisor.

I would find it very difficult if I had a supervisor who as it were dismissed the spiritual element completely or always wanted to psychologize everything.

Again, in the second study I found examples of tensions within the supervisory relationship around spirituality. One solution of course is for the therapist to seek a supervisor familiar with, and open to, the part played by spirituality in therapy. However, this option is not always practical, and in some counselling agencies therapists may be assigned supervisors or have limited choices. For trainee therapists the situation can be even worse. A failure in the supervision relationship may be taken as a lack of competence in the trainee, or certainly the trainee may feel this to be the case. For a further discussion of these issues see West (1999c).

CASE EXAMPLES

To bring out the issues involved whilst working with spiritual interventions, spiritual unfolding and spiritual experiences with clients it seems helpful to present some examples from my work as a therapist and as a supervisor of therapists. (For some fascinating examples from within an American context see Richards and Bergin, 1997, Chapter 11.)

Before I present these case examples it is worth reflecting on the implications and limitations of the use of case studies and examples within therapy literature. As Totton and Edmondson state:

> It's always good fun to read about a therapist's clients and their sessions – as good as a novel – and in some ways it is very informative. But it is also very easy – in fact, inevitable – to over-simplify the wholeness of a person's life and struggle. (1988: 3–4)

So what I will include here will be extracts taken somewhat out of context, with some of the details changed to preserve confidentiality, with the aim of illustrating the possibilities of spiritual interventions and of regarding the therapy space as a spiritual space.

My own approach to therapeutic work with clients has since the mid 1980s evolved away from being overly focused on dramatic forms of cathartic therapy or healing, away from doing towards being, focusing on the client unfolding and an increasing awareness that this unfolding needed to be seen as spiritual.

If we are to work with this process of the unfolding in our clients then there seems to me a need for a great sense of trust, a trust in the process if you like; or to put it into Julian of Norwich's words, 'All will be well' (Jantzen, 1987), perhaps a hard philosophy to adopt in a world full of so much pain and suffering. However, this being with our clients does seem to make sense, does seem to deliver results. Paradoxically, allowing things to unfold takes great skill. It is a lot easier to choose some technique to make things happen and indeed many clients may need or demand just that. It is a kind of skill restraint reminiscent of Taoism:

> Hence the sage says, I take no action and the people are transformed of themselves
> I prefer stillness and the people are rectified of themselves. (Lao Tzu, 1963: 118)

It also demands a high quality of supervision, by a supervisor not put off by spirituality.

Case 1

The value of allowing the client to unfold their process in what is felt to be a spiritual context and trusting the unfolding is illustrated by a client who came to me in the early 1990s. He was in his mid 20s and had taken time off work as he was clearly in a deep crisis. He was staying with a close friend of his who lived in the same city as me. There were several themes he explored during a four-week period of seeing me twice a week. One was a change, development and maturing of his sexual desires; another was a shift from comparative success in the world of business towards wanting to do caring work with people. Underlying this change of his was a deep, though mostly implicit, feeling of a spiritual shift. There were intense times of grief and self-questioning for him. My part as his counsellor was to be present for him, to be an anchor during his time of change and turbulence, a witness and a sounding board. He did the work, much of it outside the counselling sessions. Looking back, this client was clearly passing through a time of spiritual emergence as described by Grof and Grof (1989).

Case 2

More recently I was presented with a different challenge from a coun-selling client. She was an ex-member of a Buddhist group which appeared to act as some kind of sect or cult in a way that I found was contrary to my understanding of Buddhism. However, I had to put my prejudices aside and listen to her ambivalence about leaving the group, about what had been good and creative and indeed spiritual for her within that group, and what had been painful and unhelpful. She was also faced with a lack of a spiritual home and whether in leaving the group she was someone con-demned to a Buddhist equivalent of hell.

My approach to working with her was to give her the opportunity to explore her experiences within the sect, her thoughts and feelings about her life with them (it was a residential community) and her reactions on leaving and now being in the outside world. I also sought to be accepting of her spiritual side (even though I only have limited knowledge of Buddhism and its tenets) and how she would engage with her spirituality in her world outside the community. It was a painful, questioning time for her as she adjusted to her new life outside the Buddhist community.

Case 3

Another client recently was torn between a difficult unhappy marriage he was committed to and his desire to become a monk. It would be very easy, too easy, to support him in the apparently more spiritual path of becoming a monk and the resultant celibate and simple lifestyle. However, it became clear to him, in exploring what was happening to him and the meaning attached to the experiences in his life, that his desire to become a monk was currently much more based on a desire to run away from the difficulties of his marriage. For he was unconsciously playing out with his wife some key issues from his childhood relationship with his mother, and his apparent call to become a monk was not yet deeply spiritual. At a key moment in his therapy he was challenged to explore his current predicament within the light of his Buddhist faith. This, although not an easy process for him, allowed him to gain a clearer perspective on the dilemmas that he faced.

Clearly in working with our clients' spiritual issues we need to retain the depth of our understanding of the therapeutic process and the unexamined lives we often lead. Sometimes sexuality is a flight from spirituality, sometimes vice versa. Sometimes these things are multilayered and it takes time to reach the truth. Truth itself can change, evolve and develop over time; and in our postmodern world, truth as something out there eternal and unchanging has been increasingly challenged. At the heart of a sexual encounter can be a deep sense of spirituality (perhaps we can paraphrase Carl Rogers and say: 'When I am being most physical I may be being my most spiritual') and again vice versa for it can be all of a psychospiritual unity.

Case 4

Some years ago I worked with a woman who had been 'in recovery' from alcoholism for 10 years, who had sought me out as a therapist because she knew I worked with spirituality. Suddenly a crisis had blown up for her and she once more turned to drugs and alcohol to get by. She quickly realized that this was not the way forward for her and came to me for therapy knowing something of my commitment to spirituality. Huge changes were occurring in her life: the ending of a long-term relationship, a forthcoming house move, the final daughter leaving home, trouble at work which would result in her quitting. She was encouraged by my suggesting that what was happening to her could be understood in Grof and Grof's (1989) concept of 'spiritual emergence' or 'emergency'. I chose to speak to her in these terms because when she first came for therapy she herself spoke of her spirituality and how important it was to work with a therapist who acknowledged spirituality.

She told me that she felt that part of her was absent. This was the bit that represented her knowing, her soul, and on deeper reflection she realized it was not absent but just very small and needed an opportunity to grow. This soul of hers was present in and after her crisis that led her into therapy and led her at the time of her crisis to give herself over to God. At that time I had an image of her both as a person in convalescence and also as a foetus awaiting birth. She felt it was easier and safer for her to feel 'down', since feeling good was too risky.

As her therapy unfolded and painful stories of her early life emerged she felt as if she was sifting the soil, 'clearing the rubbish, weeds, and old bedsteads from the garden' in her words, and also 'letting the poison come out'. She felt that her 'inner child' was to be found hidden in a cave in this garden. Even with such insight she still experienced despair two or three times a week and had thoughts of taking drugs or an overdose. Support from other recovering alcoholics remained crucial to her. She asked me poignantly if her times of despair would ever go away. I had to be honest and say I did not know, but perhaps if she continued to progress they would happen less often and would last for shorter times. She accepted this likely truth which was borne out by her subsequent progress. Around this time she became angry with me because she wanted me 'to work harder' and to 'make her better'. I checked out with her if there were any ways I could work harder for her. Exploring her anger further she identified other people she was angry with, and how she was afraid of their anger which would shut her up.

Starting a new relationship, it was important for her to be emotionally honest with her new partner. This proved difficult especially as she was frightened of men when they were angry with her. Sharing her despair with her new partner was something of a breakthrough for her, and although she was now emotionally more volatile she seemed to have the strength to deal with her new relationship and with her mother and daughters in a way that reflected her newly developing sense of her self.

Towards the end of her therapy sessions with me she was able to acknowledge the benefits of her work and felt she was through the worst of it, 'over the rapids' in her own words. Even so she spoke of having days when things felt bad, of a wish to have had her children with someone she loved, and how she could forgive her younger self but still had to face the consequences of her earlier life.

I felt very much in the role of witness to her struggle to come to terms with the changes in her life in a spiritually authentic way. I was able to draw on spiritual inspiration in work with her, that is allowing words and images to come to me from what I regard as a spiritual source, and sharing them with her if they felt appropriate. I felt at times like I was the port in the storm of changes in her life for her. Gradually she worked through the issues raised by these changes and found the strength to be more authentically herself.

Case 5

This case was a curious one in that it only indirectly involved the client and in fact arose with one of my supervisees some time ago. Several months into his therapy the client posed the question of why he was seeking therapy given that he was successful in his career, reasonably content in his marriage and with his children. However, something was missing in his life which suggested an existential or spiritual question. His therapist was moved to pose the question, 'What if anything does God mean to you?' This was the trigger of much exploration by the client, who had not been brought up in any religious tradition, but who had had some experiences that could be considered spiritual, e.g. a sense of oneness with all of humanity. The therapist took a very person-centred stance of travelling alongside the client in his spiritual journeying. The client was convinced that his therapist did know and could advise about his spiritual life but was deliberately withholding. The therapist insisted otherwise and maintained that it was up to the client to explore for himself with appropriate support from the therapist.

At this point one would expect the therapist's supervisor's reaction to be, 'It sounds like you are appropriately helping your client to explore the significance of what might be seen by him as a spiritual experience. You are also quite rightly challenging his view of you as a spiritual adviser or guru.' However, the reaction of this therapist's supervisor was to say, 'Either you stop this spiritual work with this client or cease supervision with me.' Despite many efforts on the part of the therapist to get to the bottom of this issue, his supervisor remained adamant in his view of this therapeutic work as being 'out of order'. Eventually the therapist involved came to me for supervision, and after considering what had happened with his previous supervisor we established a new supervisory relationship.

I remain perplexed by the attitude of his previous supervisor since I cannot see any inappropriate behaviour by the therapist with this client. Indeed, it seemed apparent that he was carefully avoiding being drawn into the role of spiritual adviser or guru to his client. I wondered what the problem was for his supervisor and how accepting his supervisor would probably have been if the client involved had been exploring issues around his sexuality rather than his spirituality. However, I can acknowledge how honest the supervisor was in saying, 'I cannot supervise you if the therapeutic work with this client continues to focus on his spirituality.'

These cases, then, illustrate some of the possibilities and problems arising in allowing spirituality to take its place within the therapy relationship. This whole chapter has focused on the practicalities of bringing a spiritual perspective into the therapy relationship. We will now consider the criticism that can be made against the thesis of this book before turning to a view of the future implications of spirituality within psychotherapy.

8

Answering the Critics

> Buber was short with unkempt hair and a long white beard – a reincarnation of some Old Testament prophet. I remember distinctly one second of the evening. He was standing at the lectern and had been going on about the human condition, God and the Covenant with Abraham, when suddenly he grasped the large, weighty Bible before him with both hands, raised it as high as possible above his head, smashed it down on the lectern and, standing with his arms outstretched, exclaimed, 'What good is that Book to us, after the Extermination Camps!' (Laing, 1985: 128–9)

So far we have considered the arguments for the acceptance and inclusion of spirituality within psychotherapy, especially when spirituality is important or problematic for the client. There are plenty of dissenting voices to be heard, beginning with Freud. It is very easy to hold to a particular viewpoint, especially when one feels passionate about it, and to deny that any truth could reside in those taking an opposing position. However, there is much to be learnt from a careful consideration of critics of the basic theme of this book: that therapists can benefit their clients by being open to the healthy aspects of spirituality within their own and their clients' lives. Rather than consider each critic in term, which itself could result in another book, I will address what seems to be the key questions and challenges presented.

1 'Spiritual questions are only existential questions in any case'

> Is spirituality the answer to the existential dilemma?
> Is existentialism the answer to the spiritual dilemma?
> (conversation with my colleague Dr Henry Hollanders)

This leads us back to the question of what spirituality is. Certainly spirituality does address much of the same territory as existentialism, dealing as it does with questions of meaning, of life and death, loss and suffering. Whether such questions are seen within therapy as spiritual and/or existential rather depends on the viewpoint of the individual client. It is also worthy of note how a number of existential writers and therapists have adopted a spiritual perspective including Martin Buber (1970) and Victor Frankl (1973). Spiritual questions sometimes are experienced by clients as existential questions. However, issues around spirituality can arise from other areas of concern besides existential issues, for example the issues that arise when clients have spiritual experiences.

2 All you need to do is offer Rogers's core conditions, or to free associate, or whatever

Such a comment comes from therapists who hold that they work with all their clients in the same way using basically the same technical approach. Whilst this is doubtlessly true for a number of therapists it does not rule out the fact that religion and spirituality are important areas of concern for many clients, and to merely insist that one's usual therapeutic approach is sufficient is to deny the knowledge base necessary to work effectively with clients around such issues. For example no competent therapist would, I imagine, deny the necessity to be sufficiently informed about sexual abuse, human development, adult sexuality and relating and so on. The same is true, I maintain, for religion and spirituality: hence this book.

3 If the client wants to explore their spirituality, fine, but I am not a priest

This is a comfortable position to take, especially by therapists not open to such exploring by their clients. However, we may reflect on the fact that many clients present issues and experiences that their therapists have never had, for example therapist and client having different genders, cultures, sexual orientation, drug experiences and so on. This does not as a rule lead the therapist to refuse to work with clients who have had different experiences to their own. So why not work with clients who wish to explore their spirituality in a therapeutic rather than a religious setting?

Also this attitude points to a narrow view of spirituality as equated with organized religion. Presumably a client who wanted to work with a priest would have already made such a choice. It is of course possible that a client's therapeutic work around spirituality issues would reach a point where *they* felt the need of a priest.

4 Freud was right, religion is at best a crooked cure

We explored some of Freud's ideas of religion in Chapter 1. Freud did acknowledge that religion has some answers to the problems of living, but as far as he was concerned religion is at best a crooked cure (quoted in Hay, 1982). Symington suggests that Freud's stance on religion stemmed from a 'passionate hatred of Judaism and of Catholicism as he knew it in *fin-de-siècle* Vienna' (1994: 62).

We can of course turn this statement on its head, and say that psycho-analysis is at best a crooked cure in dealing with the totality of, and issues arising from, human spiritual development. It is a question of perspective.

This is somewhat implied in Ken Wilber's model of human spiritual development (discussed in Chapter 6) in which Wilber maintains that secular therapy including psychoanalysis does not work with the spiritual stages of development that occur above the stage of body/mind integration.

5 Therapy is a value-free activity

There is now evidence that the majority of therapists do believe that certain values promote mental health and that these values should be endorsed and used to guide therapy. (Richards and Bergin, 1997: 47)

To maintain that therapy is a value-free activity is a comfortable stance to take. This position holds that whatever the client wants to explore is fine by the therapist who is there to help such exploring. Such a view can arise from a mistaken view of Rogers's core conditions and of his earlier labelling of his therapy as 'non-directive'. All therapists have values which guide and influence their work, indeed Rogers himself has been well criticized for holding an overly positive view of human nature (see for example May, 1982). Therapists' values guide their work and increasingly it is seen to be the case that therapy is not and cannot be a value-free activity. Indeed there are clear signs of Judaeo-Christian values to be found within therapy even by those who proclaim their work to be secular (see for example Kirschner, 1996).

6 Many religiously founded voluntary therapy organizations end up as secular

There does seem at times to be a 'takeover' of pastoral care by therapeutic culture and therapyspeak. Many voluntary organizations that often predate the founding of the British Association for Counselling seem to have lost something of the spiritual and religious inspiration of their founders as they follow the path towards a more professional but also more secular style of counselling or therapy.

One such group is the Westminster Pastoral Foundation (WPF) which still attracts many spiritually minded trainees because of the word 'pastoral' in its title. It was set up in 1965 by Bill Kyle, a Methodist minister, and by 1990 had grown into a national network of over 50 centres (Lyall, 1995). However, although in its earliest years the overtly religious element in its training courses was strong, it became increasingly psychotherapeutic, such that: 'as the 1970s wore on, many religious professionals found in WPF a way of moving towards a largely or entirely secular career, and secular professionals found a new field in which to teach and develop their expertise' (Black, 1991: 61, quoted in Lyall, 1995).

Lyall (1995) summarizes the ongoing debate within the WPF of the use and meaning of the word 'pastoral', which by 1991 had been dropped from descriptions of WPF work, which is now called psychotherapy or psychodynamic counselling (Black, 1991). Lyall concludes: 'in an emphasis on the clinical at the expense of the pastoral, something of value may be lost' (1995: 82).

7   Spirituality does not exist, you cannot measure it, you cannot research it

The same may be said to apply to love, but most people insist that love is real, is important, and has a key impact on their lives. Spirituality is alive and important to, at the very least, a significant minority of people in the world, and even in our modern technological society it does not seem to be disappearing as was expected. Clearly spirituality is an important element in many people's lives, however difficult it is for them to define. Consequently it is worthy of study and has been studied from within a number of academic disciplines.

There is growing evidence of the benefit to health of spiritual experiences and spiritual development. Correlations have been demonstrated between: having spiritual experiences and well-being (Hay, 1982; Hay and Morisy, 1978), personal flexibility and spiritual experiences (Thomas and Cooper, 1980), self-esteem and religious faith (Forst and Healey, 1990), and having divine relations (that is claims of contact with God) and well-being (Pollner, 1989). Religious experiences can also be interpreted as a self-healing mechanism (Valla and Prince, 1989). The modern study of religion and spirituality is often held to have begun with the pioneering work of William James (1901) into religious experience.

8   Once you allow religion in you lose your objectivity and impose your values on your clients

I have argued above that therapists have values which they inevitably bring to their work with their clients. It is so easy to maintain the illusion that one is objective and detached, and open to one's client's experiences. However, no work with people, whether it is research or offering therapy or other forms of care, can ever be done from a totally detached position. Indeed, to be detached is itself a position, a value, and the imposition of a lack of real engagement. We can as fellow humans never be outside our interactions with other humans. We are therefore always subjective, and the question then remains – do we adopt a critical, reflective stance in relation to this subjectivity? Indeed many therapeutic approaches, especially of a humanistic or analytic nature, rely on making use of the therapist's subjective reactions to his or her clients, which will probably be called countertransference in analytic circles or congruence in person-centred circles. (I have elsewhere discussed the issue of critical subjectivity within qualitative counselling research: see West, 1998c.)

9 People need help, not religion

This is definitely true, if by religion in this context one means the imposition of a particular faith viewpoint on the client regardless of their own opinions. There are however situations in which clients will actively seek therapeutic or other help from people of the same faith and Church as themselves. Richards and Bergin (1997) discuss the question of using denominationally specific interventions which they believe can enhance therapists' effectiveness with some clients. They distinguish this from using a more general ecumenical stance with clients of a differing religious stance to the therapist. A denominationally specific therapist 'may also become more directive, challenging, and educational in their style' (1997: 121). This can only be achieved with clients where there is sufficient trust and understanding on the part of the client in the therapist's grasp of their faith position. Richards and Bergin (1997) also suggest that such an approach not be used without a careful spiritual assessment that should confirm that the therapist does understand the client's beliefs; that the client has clearly consented to such an approach; and that the client has a potentially healthy spiritual attitude and is capable of addressing the issues so raised.

10 Clients should be listened to, not preached at

I would hope that this goes without saying. Brian Thorne (1991) has spoken of his reluctance and tentativeness at being fully spiritually alive with his clients for fear of being seen to be evangelizing. However, without turning into a preacher there are moments of inspiration or what Carl Rogers referred to as 'presence' (see discussion in Chapter 2) where therapists seem moved to speak on occasions quite forcefully to their clients. One of the Quaker therapists I interviewed (West, 1998a) spoke of this kind of experience as follows: 'There were almost tangible moments in my counselling where I was being talked through . . . I suddenly seemed to speak very pointedly to my clients, and afterwards, when I heard the echo of myself spoken, I thought, "Wow, did I say that?"'

In this context it is important to acknowledge that some forms of 'Christian counselling' are Bible based and explicitly use Christian teaching. For instance in an interview in a recent edition of *Carer and Counsellor*, an explicitly Christian publication, the US psychologist Larry Crabb states:

> When a patient goes to see a therapist, he's really asking the therapist to do the sanctifying work that the Spirit of God does through His Word. In the end, all counselling – intentionally or not – deals with issues of sanctification. The primary context for healing, then, should be the Christian community, not the antiseptic world of a private-practice therapist. (Crabb and Miller, 1996: 16)

11   No-one expects their GP to be religious, so why their therapist?

Perhaps no-one does expect their GP to be religious, although there is huge interest and debate within the health service about spirituality and the spiritual care of patients and what this means if it is not left entirely to the hospital chaplain to offer. This has been a feature of Project 2000 in the UK, which has contributed to changes in the nursing care of patients. Therapists in any case have a different role from GPs who usually spend less than 15 minutes with their patients, during which time they aim to complete a diagnosis of the patient's problems. The arguments advanced in this book are not about therapists being religious *per se* but more about therapists being open to the spiritual realm in whatever form if any it occurs to their clients.

12   Religion is best left to theologians

If the theologians were getting it right, perhaps this would be appropriate, but clearly in Britain many people's spiritual lives are developing outside the Churches and theology. This is not to say that therapists cannot learn something from theologians and vice versa, and one such meeting place occurs within the Association for Pastoral Care and Counselling and through its various publications. Religion and spirituality are in fact much too important to be left to theologians. Although there is perhaps only a limited interest in discussing theological dogma it is very apparent from even a brief glance at the newspapers and popular magazines that spirituality remains very important to many people.

13   What is all the fuss about? Spirituality is only part of life

True, albeit an important part. However, the continuing interest in matters of spirituality together with the decline in traditional religion in Britain highlights how much change and uncertainty is present for many people around religion and spirituality, suggesting that it will continue to arise within therapy as an issue unless therapists act to block its exploration by their clients.

Clients come to therapy because they have difficulties. Postmodern life can so easily become fragmented and many clients' therapeutic journeys seem to be about recovering meaning in their lives, and achieving some measure of integration and coherence. Spirituality can be and is an important part of that process for many people.

14   Religion and therapy do not fit together

This does seem to be many people's experience – that religion and therapy are polar opposites or are in some kind of antagonistic relationship. However, whatever model(s) of therapy, of spirituality we work to as therapists, the key matter is our clients and how they make sense of the world. Working on the relationship between spirituality and therapy may well be a key feature of some clients' work and it is important that their therapists can travel alongside them.

Maybe in some important sense therapy and spirituality do not fit together but they both deal with many overlapping key features of human existence, and fundamentally neither can or should ignore the other, or engage in infantile polemics.

15 Religion is a defence

Spirituality like sexuality can be used as a defence against feelings and against experiences we would rather not have. A skilled therapist can explore such a defence to enable the client to choose whether they need such a defence any longer. This could well result in the client having access to a deeper sense of themselves and their inner truth. In such a therapeutic process with the appropriate dissolving of the religious defence a truer, more real sense of spirituality could be revealed.

16 Religion is unhealthy, indeed destructive for some individuals

There are many examples of people who have become mentally ill, in some cases criminally insane, in which religious beliefs have played a key part in these developments. It is very noticeable that there are parallels between what can lead to a mystical experience and to a psychotic episode, for example lack of sleep and fasting. We have already explored the diagnostic difficulties in distinguishing the two in Chapter 6.

17 Most spirituality is pseudo-spirituality

This is the position of Krishnamurti (1975), among others, who argued that any path of technique takes one away from spirituality by becoming an end in itself. Somewhat similarly organized, religion can become a social club or a ritual. This is no bad thing in itself, but in the process the spiritual may get lost. However, there is profound hope latent in this proposition that if one drops the props of pseudo-spirituality then a real spirituality can become manifest. Many people following a New Age spiritual path (as discussed in Chapter 4) avoid any form of organized religion which they view as an impediment to their own spiritual development.

There is a tension within Christianity between the charismatic and Pentecostal churches (growing in numbers) who hold that the Holy Spirit is available and can be experienced frequently acting in believers' lives, and those who worship a more remote, less personal God who does not take such an active part in human affairs.

18   Religion causes more problems than it solves

There is much truth in this statement: witness the Inquisition, the Crusades, the persecution of witches, and the continuing role of many faiths in legitimizing warfare. However, because religion is so tarnished it does not mean it is therefore worthless. Like science, religion has also given much that is good to the world despite its many failures. Indeed, a similar argument could be advanced against therapy (Hillman and Ventura, 1992).

Human beings are imperfect creatures capable of great compassion and terrible cruelty. Religion, like science and therapy, however inspired, is a human invention and consequently and inevitably incomplete. Although religion so often fails, or rather its exponents are all too human and fallible, that does not make the spiritual path a worthless route to pursue. Maybe we need a new human construct to take the place of religion and spirituality which deals with something of the same territory but in a new way, less leaden with history. On the other hand the word 'spiritual' does spring readily to people's lips to explain or convey the inexplicable special sensation and feelings associated with a spiritual experience, with a sense of being part of something bigger, something greater than their usual sense of self. It is hardly surprising that such experiences often change people for the better.

In this chapter then we have been listening to, and answering, the critics of the thesis of this book about therapists being open to spirituality in their clients and in themselves. It has at times been an uncomfortable experience viewing the weak points in this argument that spirituality is important and meaningful in many people's lives. In the next chapter we consider some of what the future holds if we assume therapy is a spiritual process.

9

The Future of Therapy as a Spiritual Activity

> My struggle to integrate my therapeutic work with my spiritual and religious life reflects the preoccupations of many of my fellow professionals and not a few of my co-religionists. (Thorne, 1998: ix–x)

> However, it is important not to underestimate the deep anxieties that can arise when counsellors try to work with both the religious and psychological paradigms together. (Rose, 1996: 18)

Spirituality has been part of human life since time immemorial and it is recognized by many people as relevant in some way to their lives. As Lyall puts it:

> The spiritual journey of the client is nearly always a reflection of important themes in that person's life. It is surely a paradox that, in an age when the most intimate details of a client's family and sexual history are openly discussed, there should be a reticence about exploring details of the faith journey. (1995: 84)

How much longer can psychotherapy and counselling ignore the healthy as well as the possibly pathological part that spirituality plays in our lives? It is time for therapists and their trainers and supervisors to relate to the reality of their clients' spiritual lives, and to look beyond any prejudices and countertransference reactions they might have relating to religion and spirituality.

Of course this does not have to be choosing either secular therapy, or therapy with a spiritual perspective, or religion with a therapeutic perspective. It is possible to work with the uncertainty involved, particularly if that is how the client perceives it. A phenomenological approach as advocated in Chapter 6 allows for the possibility that there are new formulations possible. Certainly the therapeutic and spiritual needs of the many people in Britain having spiritual experiences cannot be addressed by the Christian Churches or by many secularly minded therapists.

Both the therapeutic path and the spiritual path of discovery are too often discussed in terms of suffering of pain, anger, rage, fear and hatred. The spiritual path can involve the bliss of the spiritual experience and both paths can have moments of real meeting and real intimacy. An inclusive therapeutic approach open to the client's spirituality however expressed would certainly have room for joy and bliss.

THE MEETING PLACE AND THE DIFFERENCE BETWEEN SPIRITUAL DIRECTION AND THERAPY

It is doubtless true how much modern therapy has impacted on the Christian Churches and other religions. Indeed Lyall (1995) points out how religion has taken the modern therapies into itself and incorporated them into its ministry of pastoral care. Counselling and psychotherapy, though embarrassed at times by their religious origins, can be understood as an embodiment of largely Judaeo-Christian ethics and values. Kirschner (1996) explores the Judaeo-Christian roots of modern psychoanalysis and argues that modern ideas of the self are not new.

Not all of those involved with spiritual direction are entirely happy with the influx of therapy into spiritual direction. Kenneth Leech (1994) offers us a challenging critique of what is lost if a spiritual director (or 'soul friend' in his telling phrase) embraces modern therapeutic structures and techniques at the expense of more traditional pastoral approaches. If we do have a God shaped hole inside us, or a spiritual need, then secular therapy and psychology have no complete answer to the human condition. We are then left like Jung, recognizing the need for a religious cure to what ails us.

Spiritual direction in its Christian form is about the relationship between the person and the divine. In the meeting between director and directee there is a third presence – that of God or the spiritual. No longer is it the two people in the room of the psychotherapy relationship. This potentially changes everything. Indeed many would insist that the spiritual director is not the director, that this presence is in Christianity the work of the Holy Spirit (Jeff, 1987).

Drawing on the work of Lyall (1995) and Leech (1994) among others, I have summarized the main features of spiritual direction and therapy in Table 9.1. There could possibly be a third category of pastoral counselling, but that would only confuse the issue and raise questions as to whether it was use of secular counselling by a religious leader, or guidance based on holy text and faith. Perhaps the two columns of therapy and spiritual direction in the table can be taken as end points of a spectrum. I am aware that this table reflects the Christian view of spiritual direction and its relationship with therapy.

Veness (1990) suggests that counsellors, although focusing mainly on psychological growth and integration, should be comfortable within the spiritual dimension. Likewise the spiritual director who is there to guide individuals on their spiritual journey should also have some knowledge of psychological difficulties that can arise on that journey. She goes further

Table 9.1 *Comparing therapy and spiritual direction*

Psychotherapy and counselling	Spiritual direction
Helping and supportive relationship with agency or professional context	Helping and supportive relationship in a faith context
One-to-one or group	One-to-one or group
Client has emotional or psychological distress	Client may not have a crisis
clinic or office based	Based in a community of faith
Can be seen as helping client adjust to society	Helps clients lead a life of faith
Focus on mental and emotional dimensions	Focus on spiritual issues including: prayer life, religious experiences and relationship to God
Aims to strengthen client's autonomy	Aims to self-surrender to the will of God
Often formal hourly sessions over weeks, months or years	Sometimes informal, periodic or intensive (e.g. retreats)

and insists that 'a separation of the two roles can result in an artificial break in what should be a continuum of experience' (1990: 259).

This coming together of the two roles may represent for Christianity a return to its soul care roots, but in other traditions there is little secular therapy to be found. For example, therapy may be provided by the guru for those of a Hindu faith, and in Japan, for instance, therapy is offered by Buddhist monks or Shinto priests.

Jill Hall takes Veness's argument a stage further as she proposes:

I see counselling as an interchange between two people incorporating all levels of being: the sharing of concerns and worries, fears and hopes, successes and failures, agonies and joys, in such a way that it becomes possible to experience the interchange as soul speaking with soul. (1990: 280)

Here perhaps we are seeing the emergence of therapists potentially able to work with their clients with most if not all of Wilber's 10 levels of human spiritual development.

ADDRESSING THE HOLISTIC TOTALITY OF PEOPLE'S LIVES

One of the dangers of modern health care is the increasing specialism, so that one consults a bewildering range of specialists who are concerned with a small part or aspect of one's being. It seems less and less possible to have a consultation with a health professional outside the complementary medicine field which even attempts to be holistic. If we accept that people are physical, emotional, mental and spiritual beings, then somehow this reality needs addressing, certainly as part of a process of healing. This could be where the truly holistic therapist could come in as long as she or he was not afraid to address the reality of the spiritual in their clients, and their own lives.

It does not end however with addressing the holistic totality of one's client's life, for one's clients live on planet earth. Once we begin to accept the spiritual totality of our lives we cease to regard each other, all of life, and the planet as separate. Working with our clients spiritually can result in engaging in something akin to I–Thou relating. This means being open to how much our clients change us by who they are and the issues they explore in therapy. It also involves recognizing the reality of the 'in-between', that there are ways in which we will experience ourselves as no longer separate from our clients, and in those moments there are often profound possibilities of healing for them and for us. Such spiritual experiencing is life changing.

This view is reflected in the comments made by one of the participants in my research into therapy and healing (West, 1995a): 'I don't experience myself and other people as separate, and although I work with individuals I'm always aware of the interconnection.' This is reminiscent of the view expressed by Capra (1982) and Sheldrake (1994), amongst others, that people are interconnected with each other and with creation, and that the denial of such interconnectedness can be seen as a prime cause of our neurosis. Indeed, experiencing such interconnectedness can sometimes be frightening, and it can also very often prove to be of a spiritual healing nature. As another of my therapy and healing respondents said:

> The aim of my work is not just to help people change whatever it is they don't feel happy with, and it isn't just to help people thrive in the 'here and now'. It's to help them to see for themselves, feel for themselves their eternal issues, in a bigger context to say the least.

This bigger context in therapeutic terms can be seen as the spiritual space explored in Chapter 5.

Of course, there is the possibility of the downside or even shadow side to such experiences of interconnectedness. Within Gestalt therapy (Clarkson, 1989; Perls, 1969a; 1969b) there is the concept of confluence, in which there is a loss of boundaries between two people such that one may decide to surrender their autonomy and say in effect, 'I want whatever you want.' This is clearly not the reality of the I–Thou encounter but confusion between the two is no doubt possible.

SUPERVISION DILEMMAS

I have discussed in Chapter 7 some of the supervision difficulties that might arise when therapists' work with their clients embraces the spiritual. These difficulties centred around the supervisor not being open to and valuing the spiritual. It is worth considering the possible solutions to these problems. These to my mind number six. (This whole area is explored in greater detail in West, 1999c.)

The first solution, which is really no solution at all since it is ethically unacceptable, is that of *ignoring or playing down spirituality* and its part in the client's therapy. Apart from the risk that this places the client in, it also will tend to undermine the supervision relationship in the whole of the therapy work supervised and will create incongruence in that relationship.

A second solution is that of *using two supervisors*, one to supervise the counselling/psychotherapy, the other to supervise the part of the therapy where spirituality is a prominent feature. However, problems immediately arise. How do you split the individual session for supervision? How can the therapist deal with what might be conflicting advice from the two supervisors (does this result in a classic split of good supervisor and bad supervisor)? How can the therapy supervisor make sense of the impact of the possible spiritual intervention on the client? Clearly this is an unworkable solution.

A third and potentially more satisfying solution, at least to the stretched supervisor, would be to *confine the therapeutic work within a therapy boundary and limit the spiritual work to other helping relationships with their own forms of supervision and guidance*. This is an apparently neat solution to many of the dilemmas explored earlier. However, clients often find out or seek out spiritually inclined therapists. To deny clients what we know in our hearts to be valuable and potentially very helpful for them is to my mind unethical. This not to say that we should routinely offer spiritual interventions to clients who have not sought them. That is another matter.

A fourth possible solution would be to *find a supervisor who has experience of the use of spirituality within therapy*. This solution was adopted by the Gestalt therapist mentioned in Chapter 6 who had a supervisor who was also a priest. This was especially helpful in dealing with what appeared to be ghosts in the therapy room. The supervisor encouraged the therapist not to foreclose on the decision of whether the entities were of a spiritual or a psychological nature. They could be worked with therapeutically in either case.

This solution may not work since what we are talking about is how to bring spirituality within the therapy frame, and there are various ways in which this can be achieved. Nevertheless this solution might well turn out to be the best fit that is available.

A fifth solution is to seek *further training in a religiously or spiritually based form of therapy*, e.g. some version of Christian counselling which would limit possible client choices, or to train in transpersonal, psychosynthesis, Jungian or other spiritually based forms of therapy. This is an attractive solution and would hopefully deal with the supervision dilemma. It does, however, represent a whole new school of therapy which may lead to integration issues for an already trained therapist who will then have to choose which school to belong to or attempt their own personal integration.

A final possible solution is *to accept that these dilemmas have no neat solutions*, and to work with the issues in the supervisory relationship as did a number of therapists discussed in Chapter 7.

It is also clear that the five ethical solutions presented do not always work (we can ignore the first, unethical solution). When we have such an eminent counsellor as Brian Thorne (1991) talking of having to leave his soul outside the counselling room door, perhaps we are dealing with something that does not always permit an easy solution.

ETHICAL AND BOUNDARY ISSUES

So far this book has addressed the cultural, theoretical and practice issues that can arise when the world of therapy is willing to acknowledge the spiritual as an important and potentially healthy part of many people's lives. However, once a therapist chooses to recognize spirituality as relevant to therapeutic practice, a number of issues arise, many of which are of an ethical nature.

1 Is the therapist competent to work with their client around spirituality? Has she or he had sufficient training and personal development work on spirituality? If not, can she or he recognize where the boundary does lie beyond which they should not work with their client, and can this be made clear in their contracting with their clients?

2 Is the existing supervision arrangement appropriate for this new development in the therapist's work: that is, is the supervisor competent? Is the supervisor open to the therapist working in a way that includes the client's spirituality?

3 How will addressing the client's spirituality impact on the therapeutic relationship including issues around transference and countertransference, the use of congruence, disclosure and power? As we have seen in the spiritual direction relationship it is often held that God or the Holy Spirit (in Christian terms) is the director, which has implications for the kind of transference that can arise. Is the therapist willing to confront transference and countertransference issues arising when they are present in their client's spirituality?

4 How will the therapist try to ensure that any spiritual experiences that happen to the client within and outside the therapy room are beneficial to the client? The therapist's attitude to such experiences can have a crucial bearing on how easily the client can integrate such experiences.

5 How can the therapist sit comfortably with their view of spirituality alongside that of their client's? When the therapist is confronted with an unusual or new religious or spiritual perspective in a client (for example membership of a new religious movement, or a disturbing spiritual experience) then it is necessary to learn something of that perspective and to explore, outside the therapeutic relationship, her or his reactions to it.

6 Is the therapist clear about when a referral will be necessary and to whom? This could include spiritual direction by someone within the faith community of the client, it could include medical help for mental health problems, or it could be to a colleague with more experience of clients' spiritual issues.

7 Is the therapist aware of issues that might arise if the client undergoes a spiritual emergency? An exploration of the relevant literature and a discussion within supervision should help as discussed below.

8 Many believe that Brian Thorne's work with his client Sally described in a chapter from *Beyond the Core Conditions* (Thorne, 1991) is unethical in a number of ways. This case and the resultant literature is worthy of close study as part of a clarification of what is, and what is not, appropriate behaviour on the part of a therapist working with clients on matters to do with their spirituality and sexuality.

When clients explore their spirituality in therapy they are dealing with a deep and often tender part of themselves in circumstances in which they feel very open and often unbounded. It is crucial that any exploration of spirituality, whether in a religious context or a therapeutic context, is free from abuse and exploitation.

WHAT IS TO BE DONE? AN AGENDA FOR CHANGE

In Chapter 1 I put forward, in brief, what a training programme around spirituality for practising psychotherapists and counsellors should contain. It is worth revisiting this programme in the light of the discussion of ideas presented in this book.

1 Therapists' should examine their own prejudices and biases around spirituality and religion, both positive and negative.

This involves taking responsibility for countertransferences, whether of a positive or a negative variety. This inevitably should be an ongoing process as new clients raise new issues around religion and spirituality. Such exploring could arise spontaneously in supervision, or could be the focus of some individual therapy work, or a meeting with spiritual leaders, or the study of relevant literature.

2 Therapists should familiarize themselves with some of the literature around spiritual experiences and pastoral therapy and spiritual direction.

This exploration should be carried out in good faith from a position of acceptance of the possible value of such experiences to clients, a recognition that spiritual experiences correlate with mental health, and the value to a religiously inclined client of pursuing a spiritual life.

3 Therapists should explore a religion from a different culture than their own including attending a religious service.

This is a crucial point since religion has to be experienced at least to a minimal extent to be truly understandable, and to genuinely engage in such a cross-cultural spiritual experience is potentially life changing.

4   Therapists should address the assessment issues involved, including when a spiritual experience might have psychotic elements to it, when a client needs a spiritual referral and whom to refer the client on to, and the part played by spiritual emergence and spiritual emergency in some people's spiritual development.

Here an open mind and an open heart are necessary. It is not logical to deny the health in spiritual experience or to deny that occasionally a psychotic element will be involved. However, care needs to be taken to ensure that such experiences are understood within their cultural contexts.

5   Therapists should develop a sense of some of the main maps and theories of spiritual development.

There is no need to reinvent the wheel. Particular phenomena may arise at certain stages of spiritual development and a familiarity with such maps help both therapist and client. Many clients having spiritual experiences (Hay, 1982) fear they are going mad; most of them are not, and anxieties can be allayed by an informed therapist.

One of the therapists I interviewed during my research into therapy and healing (West, 1995a) spoke of how someone on a 'deep ecology' workshop had begun to exhibit psychotic features:

> It was like he'd jumped off the cliff, and he went right in and couldn't get himself out . . . He wasn't sleeping . . . Wednesday morning he accosted one of the workshop leaders . . . and fell on his knees in front of her and clasped her by the knees and said, 'Tell me how to save the planet.' Of course she reacted, this guy was very big, and he had a lot of very very powerful energy locked up inside him . . . It was like a walking time bomb.

It was clear that this man needed to be off the course and somewhere quiet, which fortunately the therapist was able to provide. Later:

> I sat down with him that evening and I gave him a book on spiritual processes – *The Handbook for People in Spiritual Emergencies* – and I said I want you to read this, especially this bit here, and it's like a description of the various types of states, and he said, 'Oh, I've got that, I've got that, oh, that's what's going on. Oh God I thought I was going crazy.'

Providing this very troubled man with an intellectual handle for his experience had helped him come to ground and begin to come to terms with it.

6   Therapists should study implicit and explicit spiritual forms of counselling.

Without having to train as a Jungian or as a transpersonal therapist etc., there is much of value that can be learnt from how such therapeutic approaches address the spiritual lives of their clients.

7   Therapists should clarify the differences and overlaps between spiritual direction, pastoral care and counselling or psychotherapy, including non-Christian forms of spiritual care.

This is a trickier issue to tease out but the effort is well worth making. The question worth asking is: at what stage, with what client, if any, would one make a referral for spiritual direction or pastoral care? In answering this question greater clarity should arise about the overlap and possible co-operation between these differing forms of helping.

8   Therapists should be engaged in their own form of spiritual development.

It seems to me unimaginable that we can engage in supporting our clients as spiritual beings without addressing our own spirituality. Any therapist unwilling to meet and acknowledge their own spiritual nature is ill equipped to be present for their client's spirituality.

9   Therapists should have appropriate supervision arrangements in place.

It should be abundantly clear from the discussion of supervision dilemmas above, and from the discussion in Chapter 7, how crucial appropriate supervision is. It is highly likely that any one supervisor will not be able to meet all of one's needs for supervision including spirituality issues. Therapists need to be aware of what their, and their supervisors', blind spots are and to seek to cover such deficiencies by further supervision and appropriate training.

Of course the training and supervisory needs of the individual therapist are only part of what is needed. Clearly the issues raised in this book need to be addressed by the wider therapeutic world in terms of courses, seminars, conferences, debates, papers, books, the whole spectrum of professional activities, some of which has already occurred. Further efforts can and should be made to take this work forward.

WIDER IMPLICATIONS

Spirituality and spiritual experiences remain part of our lives even in these postmodern times. The decline in conventional church attendance in Britain and the apparent secularization of our society could be taken as an indication that spirituality is moribund, but it is a fundamental aspect of human experience which remains important to many people and finds expression in an increasing variety of ways. A significant number of people (at least a third) continue to have spiritual experiences, which like David Hay (1982) I regard as 'biological' and to do with the very survival of our species. He suggests that the survival of our species depends on a shift away from materialism to avoid ecological collapse, and a recognition of our mutual interdependence to avoid destructive nuclear warfare. Having spiritual experiences can strengthen both. This has two implications for therapists. One is that as therapists are not, by and large, trained to work with spirituality and spiritual issues arising for their clients, they are ignoring a key element of their clients' experience which is of great relevance for their psychological health. Secondly, spiritual experiences can and will happen to therapists, possibly as a direct result of how their very work is akin to a spiritual practice.

My research into therapy and healing strengthened my belief that therapy and healing each have a particular contribution to make in alleviating the ills of the individual and of our society, and beyond. For there is a wider dimension: many healers now believe that it is hopeless to heal the individual without healing the planet (Vaughan, 1986), that the solution to the dilemma of mankind's 'empty self' (Cushman, 1990) lies in our experiencing our interconnectedness with each other and with the planet. It we accept Lovelock's (1979) Gaia thesis that the planet is a living entity then we realize that our future as a species is bound up with the health of our planet whose ecosystem is in many ways under a great strain. From such an essentially spiritual perspective, there is hope that we can face the consequences of our collective actions and inactions.

> We have become as gods with the power to destroy the world. Will we waken in time to the vision that allows us to see that we also have within us the wisdom to preserve it? . . . We must learn to apply what we know about healing ourselves to healing the planet. (Vaughan, 1986: 216)

Without wishing to sound like an ecological version of a hell and damnation Christian preacher, I do feel that healing the planet is the key issue of our time. Colin Feltham says:

> Counsellors, if they are indeed engaged in a truth-seeking venture, might be asked 'What is counselling doing in relation to the deteriorating world?' and 'May not the collective deteriorating world be more sickening to your clients than their individual psycho-archaeologies?' (1995: 3)

I realize that I am opening out the debate beyond the need for therapists to be culturally and spiritually equipped to work with their clients, which is in itself a tall order, unless we take McLeod's (1998) advice that we need a framework for understanding culture including our own, rather than attempting to understand each and every culture and subculture.

In a therapy world in which short-term and problem managing forms of counselling and psychotherapy seem to dominate, is there room for the client's spirituality? I believe there is. Certainly the models of spiritual direction and counsel within Christianity, Judaism, Islam, Hinduism and Sikhism are not dependent on regular weekly sessions. (Though regular attendance at spiritual services might well form part of the recommended treatment.)

In our postmodern world of virtual relationships, can a sense of spirituality survive and develop? There are certainly a number of active e-mail discussion lists in which religious and spiritual matters are explored, sometimes within a faith and spiritual guidance context. I am not aware as yet of any forms of spiritual therapy over the Web to match their secular counterparts.

However, the question remains: are counsellors and psychotherapists willing to address the spiritual dimensions of people's lives? If so, then therapy has an important part to play in the future of human beings and the world in which we live. If not, then it will not fulfil its full potential role, and the healing that is necessary is likely to be limited and incomplete.

References

Alexander, F. (1931) 'Buddhist training as artificial catatonia', *Psychoanalytic Review*, 18: 129–45.

Allman, L.S., De La Rocha, O., Elkins, D.N. and Weathers, R.S. (1992) 'Psychotherapists' attitudes towards clients reporting mystical experiences', *Psychotherapy*, 29 (4): 654–69.

Allport, G.W. and Ross, J.M. (1967) 'Personal religious orientation and prejudice', *Journal of Personality and Social Psychology*, 5: 432–43.

American Psychiatric Association (1994) *Diagnostic and Statistical Manual of Mental Disorders*, 4th edn (DSM-IV). Washington, DC: APA.

Assagioli, R. (1986) 'Self-realisation and psychological disturbance', *Revision*, 8 (2): 21–31.

Barker, E. (1989) *New Religious Movements: an Introduction*. London: HMSO.

Bates, B. (1993) 'Visions of reality in shamanic psychology', *Changes*, 11 (3): 223–8.

Benner, D.G. (1988) *Psychotherapy and the Spiritual Quest*. Michigan: Baker.

Bergin, A.E. (1980) 'Psychotherapy and religious values', *Journal of Consulting and Clinical Psychology*, 48: 75–105.

Bergin, A.E. and Jensen, J.P. (1990) 'Religiosity of psychotherapists: a national survey', *Psychotherapy*, 27: 3–7.

Bilgrave, D.P. and Deluty, R.H. (1998) 'Religious beliefs and therapeutic orientations of clinical and counseling psychologists', *Journal for the Scientific Study of Religion*, 37 (2): 329–49.

Black, D. (1991) *A Place for Exploration: the Story of the Westminster Pastoral Foundation 1969–1990*. London: WPF.

Boorstein, S. (ed.) (1986) *Transpersonal Psychotherapy*. Palo Alto, CA: Science and Behavior Books.

Boucouvalas, M. (1980) 'Transpersonal psychology: an outline of the field', *Journal of Transpersonal Psychology*, 12 (10): 37–46.

Brazier, D. (1996) 'A Zen response', *Self & Society*, 24 (4): 15–18.

Brierley, P. (1991) *Prospects for the Nineties: All England Trends and Tables from the English Church Census, with Denominations and Churchmanships*. London: MARC Europe.

British Association for Counselling (1996) *Code of Ethics and Practice for the Supervision of Counsellors*. Rugby: BAC.

Bruce, S. (1995a) *Religion in Modern Britain*. Oxford: Oxford University Press.

Bruce, S. (1995b) 'The truth about religion in Britain', *Journal for the Scientific Study of Religion*, 34 (4): 417–30.

Buber, M. (1970) *I and Thou* (1923). Edinburgh: Clark.

Byrd, R.C. (1988) 'Positive therapeutic effects of intercessory prayer in coronary care unit population', *Southern Medical Journal*, 81: 826–929.

Capra, F. (1982) *The Turning Point*. London: Wildwood.

Carlat, D.J. (1989) 'Psychological motivation and the choice of spiritual symbols: a case study', *Journal of Transpersonal Psychology*, 21 (2): 139–48.

Chaplin, J. (1989) 'Rhythm and blues', in W. Dryden and L. Spurling (eds), *On Becoming a Psychotherapist*. London: Tavistock/Routledge.

Clark, F.V. (1979) 'Exploring intuition: prospects and possibilities', *Journal of Transpersonal Psychology*, 5 (2): 156–70.

Clarkson, P. (1989) *Gestalt Counselling in Action*. London: Sage.

Clarkson, P. (1990) 'A multiplicity of therapeutic relationships', *British Journal of Psychotherapy*, 7 (2): 148–63.

Claxton, G. (1996) 'Therapy and beyond: concluding thoughts', in G. Claxton (ed.), *Beyond Therapy: the Impact of Eastern Religions on Psychological Theory and Practice*. Dorset: Prism.

Coleman, M.L. (1958) 'The paranormal triangle in analytic supervision', *Psychoanalysis and Psychoanalytic Review*, 45: 73–84.

Cooper, D. (1970) *Psychiatry and Anti Psychiatry*. London: Paladin.

Courtenay, A. (1991) *Healing Now*. London: Dent.

Crabb, L. and Miller, K.D. (1996) 'The end of Christian psychology?', *Carer and Counsellor*, 6 (4): 15–17.

Cushman, P. (1990) 'Why the self is empty: towards a historically situated psychology', *American Psychologist*, May: 599–611.

Dandelion, B.P. (1996) *A Sociological Analysis of the Theology of Quakers*. Lampeter: Mellen.

Davie, G. (1994) *Religion in Britain since 1945*. Oxford: Blackwell.

Deikman, A.J. (1982) *The Observing Self: Mysticism and Psychotherapy*. Boston: Beacon.

Denzin, N.K. (1989) *Interpretive Interactionism*. Newbury Park, CA: Sage.

de Silva, P. (1993) 'Buddhism and counselling', *British Journal of Guidance and Counselling*, 21 (1): 30–4.

de Silva, P. (1996) 'Buddhism and behaviour change: implications for therapy', in G. Claxton (ed.), *Beyond Therapy: the Impact of Eastern Religions on Psychological Theory and Practice*. Dorset: Prism.

DiBlasio, F.A. and Proctor, J.H. (1993) 'Therapists and the clinical use of forgiveness', *American Journal of Family Therapy*, 21 (2): 175–83.

Donington, L. (1994) 'Core process psychotherapy', in D. Jones (ed.), *Innovative Therapy: a Handbook*. Buckingham: Open University Press.

Dryden, W. and Feltham, C. (eds) (1992) *Psychotherapy and its Discontents*. Buckingham: Open University Press.

Dryden, W. and Spurling, L. (1989) *On Becoming a Psychotherapist*. London: Tavistock/Routledge.

Edwards, G. (1992) 'Does psychotherapy need a soul?', in W. Dryden and C. Feltham (eds), *Psychotherapy and its Discontents*. Buckingham: Open University Press.

Egan, G. (1990) *The Skilled Helper*, 4th edn. Pacific Grove, CA: Brooks/Cole.

Ehrenwald, J. (1954) *New Dimensions of Depth Analysis: a Study of Telepathy in Interpersonal Relationships*. London: Allen & Unwin.

Eliade, M. (1960) *Myths, Dreams and Mysteries*. New York: Harper and Row.

Eliade, M. (1964) *Shamanism: Archaic Techniques of Ecstasy*. Princeton, NJ: Princeton University Press.

Elkins, D.N., Hedstorm, L.J., Hughes, L.L., Leaf, J.A. and Saunders, C. (1988) 'Towards a humanistic-phenomenological spirituality', *Journal of Humanistic Psychology*, 28 (4): 5–18.

Ellenberger, H. (1970) *The Discovery of the Unconscious*. New York: Basic Books.

Enright, D. (1996) 'Counseling within the forgiveness triad: on forgiving, receiving forgiveness, and self-forgiving', *Counsel and Values*, 40 (2): 107–26.

Erikson, E. (1977) *Childhood and Society*. London: Paladin.

Farrow, J. (1984) 'Spirituality and self-awareness', *The Friends Quarterly*, July: 312–23.

Feltham, C. (1995) *What is Counselling?* London: Sage.

Ferguson, D.S. (ed.) (1993) *New Age Spirituality*. Louisville, KY: Westminster/John Knox.

Fielding, R.G. and Llewelyn, S. (1996) 'The new religions and psychotherapy: similarities and differences', in G. Claxton (ed.), *Beyond Therapy: the Impact of Eastern Religions on Psychological Theory and Practice*. Dorset: Prism.

Forst, E. and Healy, R.M. (1990) 'Relationship between self-esteem and religious faith', *Psychological Reports*, 67: 378.

Foskett, J. and Jacobs, M. (1989) 'Pastoral counselling', in W. Dryden, D. Charles-Richards and R. Woolfe (eds), *Handbook of Counselling in Britain*. London: Tavistock/Routledge.

Foskett, J. and Lyall, D. (1988) *Helping the Helpers*. London: SPCK.

Foundation for Inner Peace (1975) *A Course in Miracles*. Tiburon, CA: FIP.

Fowler, J.W. (1981) *Stages of Faith: the Psychology of Human Development and the Quest for Meaning*. New York: Harper and Row.

Fox, M. (1993) 'Spirituality for a new era', in D.S. Ferguson (ed.), *New Age Spirituality*. Louisville, KY: Westminster/John Knox.

Frankl, V.E. (1947) *The Unconscious God*. New York: Simon and Schuster.

Frankl, V.E. (1973) *The Doctor and the Soul: from Psychotherapy to Logotherapy*. London: Pelican.

Frankl, V.E. (1978) *Man's Search for Meaning*. London: Hodder and Stoughton.

Freud, S. (1933) *New Introductory Lectures of Psychoanalysis*. London: Hogarth.

Freud, S. (1963) *Civilization and its Discontents*. New York: Basic Books.

Friedman, M. (1993) *Religion and Psychotherapy: a Dialogical Approach*. New York: Paragon.

Fromm, E. (1950) *Psychoanalysis and Religion*. New Haven, CT: Yale University Press.

Fromm, E. (1986) *Psychoanalysis and Zen Buddhism*. London: Unwin.

Fuller, R.C. (1984) 'Rogers's impact on pastoral counseling and contemporary religious reflection', in R.F. Levant and J.M. Shlien (eds), *Client-Centered Therapy and the Person-Centered Approach*. New York: Praeger.

Gergen K.J. (1991) *The Saturated Self: Dilemmas of Identity in Modern Life*. New York: Basic Books.

Gergen, K.J. (1996) 'Postmodern society as a concept', Introductory lecture at International Conference for Psychotherapy, Vienna, July, audiotape.

Goodman, F.D. (1986) 'Body posture and the religious altered state of consciousness: an experiential investigation', *Journal of Humanistic Psychology*, 26 (3): 81–118.

Graves, R. (1961) *The White Goddess: a Historical Grammar of Poetic Myth*. London: Faber and Faber.

Greeley, A.M. (1975) *The Sociology of the Paranormal: a Reconnaissance*. Beverley Hills, CA: Sage.

Greenleaf, E. (1978) 'Active imagining', in J.L. Singer and K.S. Pope (eds), *The Power of Human Imagination: New Methods in Psychotherapy*. New York: Plenum.

Grof, C. and Grof, S. (1986) 'Spiritual emergency: the understanding and treatment of transpersonal crisis', *Revision*, 8 (2): 7–20.

Grof, S. (1972) 'Varieties of transpersonal experiences: observations from LSD psychotherapy', *Journal of Transpersonal Psychology*, 4 (1): 45–80.

Grof, S. and Grof, C. (1989) *Spiritual Emergency*. Los Angeles: Tarcher.

Guest, H. (1989) 'The origins of transpersonal psychology', *British Journal of Psychology*, 6 (1): 62–9.

Guntrip, H. (1956) *Mental Pain and the Cure of Souls*. London: Independent.

Hall, J. (1990) 'Transformation in counselling', *British Journal of Guidance & Counselling*, 18 (3): 269–80.

Hall, J.A. (1984) 'Dreams and transference/countertransference: the transformative field', *Chiron, a Review of Jungian Analysis*.

Halmos, P. (1965) *The Faith of the Counsellors*. London: Constable.

Hardy, A. (1979) *The Spiritual Nature of Man*. Oxford: Clarendon.

Hawkins, P. and Shohet, R. (1989) *Supervision in the Helping Professions*. Milton Keynes: Open University Press.

Hay, D. (1979) 'Religious experience among a group of post-graduate students – a qualitative study', *Journal for the Scientific Study of Religion*, 18 (2): 164–82.

Hay, D. (1982). *Exploring Inner Space: Scientists and Religious Experience*. Harmondsworth: Penguin.

Hay, D. and Morisy, A. (1978) 'Reports of ecstatic, paranormal, or religious experiences in Great Britain and the United States – a comparison of trends', *Journal for the Scientific Study of Religion*, 17 (3): 255–68.

Healey, B.J. (1993) 'Psychotherapy and religious experience: integrating psychoanalytic psychotherapy with Christian religious experience', in G. Stricker and J.R. Gold (eds), *Comprehensive Handbook of Psychotherapy Integration*. New York: Plenum.

Heelas, P. and Kohn, R. (1996) 'Psychotherapy and techniques of transformation', in G. Claxton (ed.), *Beyond Therapy: the Impact of Eastern Religions on Psychological Theory and Practice*. Dorset: Prism.

Hendricks, G. and Weinhold, B. (1982) *Transpersonal Approaches to Counseling and Psychotherapy*. Colorado: Love.

Herman, N. (1987) *Why Psychotherapy?* London: Free Association.

Heron, J. (1992) *Feeling and Personhood*. London: Sage.

Heron, J. (1998) *Sacred Science: Person-Centred Inquiry into the Spiritual and Subtle*. Ross-on-Wye: PCCS.

Heron, J. and Reason, P. (eds) (1985) *Whole Person Medicine*. London: British Postgraduate Medical Federation.

Hillman, J. and Ventura, M. (1992) *We've Had a Hundred Years of Psychotherapy and the World's Getting Worse*. San Francisco: Harper Collins.

Hollanders, H. (1997) 'Eclecticism/integration among counsellors in the light of Kuhn's concept of paradigm formation'. Doctoral thesis, Department of Applied Social Studies, Keele University.

Hopson, R.E. (1996) 'The 12-step program', in E.P. Shafranske (ed.), *Religion and the Clinical Practice of Psychology*. Washington, DC: American Psychological Association. pp. 533–58.

Howard, A. (1995) *Challenging Counselling and Psychotherapy*. London: Macmillan.

Hughes, G. (1989) *Getting Away from It All: a Guide to Retreat Houses and Centres for Spiritual Renewal*. Cambridge: Lutterworth.

Hurding, R. (1985) *Roots and Shoots: a Guide to Counselling and Psychotherapy*. London: Hodder and Stoughton.

Isbister, J.N. (1985) *Freud: an Introduction to his Life and Work*. Cambridge: Polity.

Jackson, M.L. (1995) 'Multicultural counseling: historic perspectives', in J.G. Ponterotto, J.M. Cases, L.A. Suzuki and C.M. Alexander (eds), *Handbook of Multi Cultural Counseling*. Thousand Oaks, CA: Sage.

James, W. (1901) *The Varieties of Religious Experience*. London: Collins.

Jantzen, G. (1987) *Julian of Norwich*. London: SPCK.

Jeff, M. (1987) *Spiritual Direction for Every Christian*. London: SPCK.

Jones, D. (1994) *Innovative Therapies: a Handbook*. Buckingham: Open University Press.

Jones, D. (1996) 'The psychospiritual: psychospiritual and transpersonal psychotherapies', *Self & Society*, 24 (4): 4–6.

Jung, C.G. (1933) *Modern Man in Search of a Soul*. London: Routledge and Kegan Paul.

Jung, C.G. (1958) *Psychology and Religion*. London: Routledge and Kegan Paul.

Jung, C.G. (1967) *Memories, Dreams, Reflections*. London: Fontana.

Jung, C.G. (1968) *Aion: Researches in the Phenomenology of the Self*. London: Routledge.

Kaberry, S. (1999) 'Abuse in supervision', in B. Lawton and C. Feltham (eds), *Taking Supervision Forward: Dilemmas, Insights and Trends*. London: Sage.

Kirschenbaum, H. and Henderson, V. (eds) (1990a) *The Carl Rogers Reader*. London: Constable.

Kirschenbaum, H. and Henderson, V. (eds) (1990b) *Carl Rogers Dialogues*. London: Constable.

Kirschner, S.R. (1996) *The Religious and Romantic Origins of Psychoanalysis*. Cambridge: Cambridge University Press.

Krippner, S. (1992) 'The shamen as healer and psychotherapist', *Voices: the Art and Science of Psychotherapy*, Winter: 12–23.

Krishnamurti, J. (1975) *Life Ahead*. New York: Harper and Row.

Kurjo, S. (1988) 'Humanistic psychology: the new global religion?', *Self & Society*, 16 (5): 229–32.

Lago, C. and Thompson, J. (1996) *Race, Culture and Counselling*. Buckingham: Open University Press.

Laing, R.D. (1967) *The Politics of Experience*. New York: Ballantine.

Laing, R.D. (1972) 'Metanoia: some experiences at Kingsley Hall, London', in H.M. Ruitenbeck (ed.), *Going Crazy*. New York: Bantam.

Laing, R.D. (1985) *Wisdom, Madness and Folly: the Making of a Psychiatrist, 1927–1957*. London: Macmillan.

Lake, F. (1981) *Tight Corners in Pastoral Counselling*. London: Darton, Longman and Todd.

Lannert, J.L. (1991) 'Resistance and countertransference issues with spiritual and religious clients', *Journal of Humanistic Psychology*, 31 (4): 68–76.

Lao, Tzu (1963) *Tao Te Ching*, trans. D.C. Lau. Harmondsworth: Penguin.

Laungani, P. (1997) 'Replacing client-centred counselling with culture-centred counselling', *Counselling Psychology Quarterly*, 10 (4): 343–51.

Lee, C.C. and Armstrong, K.L. (1995) 'Indigenous models of mental health interventions: lessons from traditional healers', in J.G. Ponterotto, J.M. Cases, L.A. Suzuki and C.M. Alexander (eds), *Handbook of Multicultural Counseling*. Thousand Oaks, CA: Sage.

Leech, K. (1994) *Soul Friend*. London: Darton, Longman and Todd.

Levy, J. (1983) 'Transpersonal and Jungian psychology', *Journal of Humanistic Psychology*, 23 (2): 42–51.

Liese, B. (1998) 'Spirituality and cognitive therapy: a match made in heaven'. Paper to Society for Psychotherapy Research (International) 29th Annual Meeting, 24–28 June, Salt Lake City.

Linehan, M. and Schmidt, H. (1995) 'The dialectics of effective treatment of borderline personality disorder', in W.T. O'Donohue and L. Krasner (eds), *Theories of Behavior Therapy: Exploring Behavior Change*. Washington, DC: American Psychological Association.

Lovelock, J. (1979) *Gaia: A New Look at Life on Earth*. Oxford: Oxford University Press.

Lovinger, R.J. (1984) *Working with Religious Issues in Therapy*. New York: Aronson.

Lukoff, D. (1985) 'The diagnosis of mystical experiences with psychotic features', *Journal of Transpersonal Psychology*, 17 (2): 155–81.

Lyall, D. (1995) *Counselling in the Pastoral and Spiritual Context*. Buckingham: Open University Press.

Mahrer, A.R. (1978) 'The therapist–patient relationship', *Psychotherapy: Theory, Research and Practice*, 15 (3): 201–15.

Mahrer, A.R. (1993) 'Transformational psychotherapy sessions', *Journal of Humanistic Psychology*, 33 (2): 30–7.

Maslow, A.H. (1970) *Religions, Values, and Peak Experiences*. New York: Viking.

May, R. (1982) 'The problem of evil: an open letter to Carl Rogers', *Journal of Humanistic Psychology*, 22 (3): 10–21.

McCullough, M.E. and Worthington, E.L. (1994) 'Models of interpersonal forgiveness and their application to counseling: review and critique', *Counseling and Values*, 39 (1): 2–14.

McFadden, J. (1996) 'A transcultural perspective: reaction to C.H. Patterson's "Multicultural counseling: from diversity to universality"', *Journal of Counseling and Development*, 74: 232–5.

McLeod, J. (1993) *Introduction to Counselling*. Buckingham: Open University Press.

McLeod, J. (1998) *Introduction to Counselling*, 2nd edn. Buckingham: Open University Press.

McNeice, M. (1996) 'Premature forgiveness', *Self & Society*, 24 (2): 11–13.

McNeill, J.T. (1951) *A History of the Cure of Souls*. New York: Harper and Row.

Mearns, D. (1994) *Developing Person-Centred Counselling*. London: Sage.

Mearns, D. and Thorne, B. (1988) *Person-Centred Counselling in Action*. London: Sage.

Mintz, E.E. (1978) 'Transpersonal events in traditional psychotherapy?', *Psychotherapy: Theory, Research and Practice*, 15 (1): 90–4.

Mollon, P. (1991) 'Psychotherapists' healing attitude'. Paper presented to Symposium on the Crucial Factor in Psychotherapy and Psychoanalysis, Department of Psychotherapy, Manchester Royal Infirmary, 9 November.

Moody, R. (1975) *Life after Life*. Atlanta: Mockingbird.

Moore, T. (ed.) (1990) *The Essential James Hillman*. London: Routledge.

Moreno, J. (1947) *The Theatre of Spontaneity*. Boston: Beacon.

Moustakas, C. (1994) *Phenomenological Research Methods*. London: Sage.

Nelson, S.H. and Torrey, E.F. (1973) 'The religious function of psychiatry', *American Journal of Orthopsychiatry*, 43: 362–7.

Norcross, J.C. and Dryden, W. (1990) *Eclecticism and Integration in Counselling and Psychotherapy*. London: Gale.

Northcott, M.S. (1992) *The New Age and Pastoral Theology: Towards the Resurgence of the Sacred*. Lightwater, Surrey: Contact Pastoral Trust.

Obeyesekere, G. (1984) *Medusa's Hair*. Chicago: University of Chicago Press.

Olds, G.A. (1993) 'The New Age: historic and metaphysical foundations', in D.S. Ferguson (ed.), *New Age Spirituality*. Louisville, KY: Westminster/John Knox.

Oxford English Dictionary (1989) Oxford: Clarendon.

Pagels, E. (1982) *The Gnostic Gospels*. Harmondsworth: Penguin.

Pahnke, W.N. and Richards, W.A. (1966) 'Implications of LSD and experiential mysticism', *Journal of Religion and Health*, 5: 176–208.

Parry, S.J. and Jones, R.G.A. (1996) 'Beyond illusion in the psychotherapeutic enterprise', in G. Claxton (ed.), *Beyond Therapy: the Impact of Eastern Religions on Psychological Theory and Practice*. Dorset: Prism.

Patterson, C.H. (1996) 'Multicultural counseling: from diversity to universality', *Journal of Counseling and Development*, 74 (1): 227–31.

Payne, I.R., Bergin, A.E. and Loftus, P.E. (1992) 'A review of attempts to integrate spiritual and standard psychotherapy techniques', *Journal of Psychotherapy Integration*, 2: 171–92.

Peck, M.S. (1990) *The Road Less Travelled: a New Psychology of Love, Traditional Values and Spiritual Growth*. London: Arrow.

Pedersen, P. (1996) 'The importance of both similarities and differences in multicultural counseling: reaction to C.H. Patterson', *Journal of Counseling and Development*, 74 (1): 236–7.

Pendzik, S. (1988) 'Drama therapy as a modern form of shamanism', *Journal of Transpersonal Psychology*, 20 (1): 81–92.

Perls, F. (1969a) *Ego Hunger and Aggression: the Beginning of Gestalt Therapy*. New York: Random House.

Perls, F. (1969b) *Gestalt Therapy Verbatim*. Lafayette, CA: Real People Press.

Peters, L.G. and Price-Williams, D. (1980) 'Towards an experiential analysis of shamanism', *American Ethnologist*, 7: 397–418.

Pietroni, P. (1993) 'The return of the spirit', in A. Beattie, M. Gott, L. Jones and M. Sidell (eds), *Health and Wellbeing: a Reader*. Milton Keynes: Open University Press.

Pollner, M. (1989) 'Divine relations, social relations, and well-being', *Journal of Health and Social Behavior*, 30: 92–104.

Ponterotto, J.G., Casas, J.M., Suzuki, L.A. and Alexander, C.M. (eds) (1995) *Handbook of Multicultural Counseling*. London: Sage.

Propst, L.R., Ostrom, R., Watkins, P., Dean, T. and Mashburn, D. (1992) 'Comparative efficacy of religious and non-religious cognitive behavioral therapy for the treatment of clinical depression in religious individuals', *Journal of Consulting and Clinical Psychology*, 60: 94–103.

Purcell-Lee, C. (1999) 'An existential approach to the therapeutic/educative relationship in the light of Buber's I–Thou/I–It distinction and his concept of inclusion'. Paper to Colloquium, Faculty of Education, Manchester University, 20 January.

Reason, P. (ed.) (1988) *Human Inquiry in Action*. London: Sage.

Reason, P. (ed.) (1994) *Participation in Human Inquiry*. London: Sage.

Reich, I.O. (1969) *Wilhelm Reich: a Personal Biography*. New York: St Martin's.

Reich, W. (1952) *The Murder of Christ*. New York: Orgone Institute Press.

Richards, P.S. and Bergin, A.E. (1997) *A Spiritual Strategy for Counseling and Psychotherapy*. Washington, DC: American Psychological Association.

Rogers, C.R. (1951) *Client-Centred Therapy: its Current Practice, Implications and Theory*. Boston: Houghton Mifflin.

Rogers, C.R. (1962) 'Some learnings from a study of psychotherapy with schizophrenics', *Pennsylvania Psychiatric Quarterly*, Summer: 3–15.

Rogers, C.R. (1980) *A Way of Being*. Boston: Houghton Mifflin.

Rose, J. (1993) 'The integration of prayer and practice in the counselling relationship'. MA thesis, Roehampton Institute of Higher Education.

Rose, J. (1996) *A Needle-Quivering Poise: between Prayer and Practice in the Counselling Relationship*. Surrey: Contact Pastoral Monograph no. 6.

Rowan, J. (1976) *Ordinary Ecstasy*. London: Routledge and Kegan Paul.

Rowan, J. (1983) 'The real self and mystical experiences', *Journal of Humanistic Psychology*, 23 (2): 9–27.

Rowan, J. (1989) 'A late developer', in W. Dryden and L. Spryling (eds), *On Becoming a Psychotherapist*. London: Tavistock/Routledge.

Rowan, J. (1993) *The Transpersonal, Psychotherapy and Counselling*. London: Routledge.

Sandford, J.A. (1993) 'Foreword', in D.S. Ferguson (ed.), *New Age Spirituality*. Louisville, KY: Westminster/John Knox.

Seymour, E. (1998) 'Towards a pagan/magickal approach to counselling'. MSc thesis, University of Bristol.

Shafranske, E.P. (1988) 'The contribution of object relations theory in Christian counseling'. Paper presented at the International Convention of Christian Psychology, Atlanta.

Shafranske, E.P. and Malony, H.N. (1985) 'Religion, spirituality, and psychotherapy: a study of Californian psychologists'. Paper presented to meeting of the California State Psychological Association, San Francisco, February.

Shafranske, E.P. and Malony, H.N. (1990) 'Clinical psychologists' religious and spiritual orientations and their practice of psychotherapy', *Psychotherapy*, 27 (1): 72–8.

Shah, I. (1969) *The Sufis*. London: Jonathan Cape.

Sheldrake, R. (1994) *Seven Experiments that Could Change the World*. London: Fourth Estate.

Sills, M. (1996) 'Psychotherapy as a spiritual journey', *Self & Society*, 24 (4): 7–14.

Skovholt, T.M. and Ronnestad, M.H. (1992) *The Evolving Professional Self: Stages and Themes in Therapist and Counselor Development*. Chichester: Wiley.

Smail, D. (1987) *Taking Care: an Alternative to Therapy*. London: Dent.

Sollod, R.N. (1978) 'Carl Rogers and the origins of client-centred therapy', *Professional Psychology*, 9: 93–104.

Spangler, D. (1993) 'The New Age: movement towards the divine', in D.S. Ferguson (ed.), *New Age Spirituality*. Louisville, KY: Westminster/John Knox.

Spanos, I. (1978) 'Witchcraft in histories of psychiatry: a critical analysis and alternative conceptualisation', *Psychological Bulletin*, 85: 417–39.

Stoltenberg, C.D. and Delworth, U. (1988) *Supervising Counselors and Therapists*. London: Jossey-Bass.

Stone, M. (1976) *The Paradise Papers: the Suppression of Women's Rites*. London: Virago.

Strupp, H.H. (1972) 'On the technology of psychotherapy', *Archives of General Psychiatry*, 26: 270–8.

Sue, D.W. and Sue, D. (1990) *Counselling the Culturally Different*, 2nd edn. New York: Wiley.

Summers, R. (1997) 'Glimpsing something of the spirit', *The Friends Quarterly*, 30 (7): 328–32.

Swinton, V. (1996) 'A study of the attitudes to the exploration of spiritual awareness in counselling training'. MA thesis, Department of Applied Social Studies, Keele University.

Symington, N. (1994) *Emotion and Spirit: Questioning the Claims of Psychoanalysis and Religion*. London: Cassell.

Szasz, T. (1988) *The Myth of Psychotherapy*. New York: Syracuse University Press.

Tart, C.T. and Deikman, A.J. (1991) 'Mindfulness, spiritual seeking and psychotherapy', *Journal of Transpersonal Psychology*, 23 (1): 29–52.

Thomas, L.E. and Brewer, S.J. (1993) 'Two patterns of transcendence: an empirical examination of Wilber's and Washbyrn's Theories', *Journal of Humanistic Psychology*, 33 (3): 66–81.

Thomas, L.E. and Cooper, P.E. (1980) 'Incidence and psychological correlates of intense spiritual experiences', *Journal of Transpersonal Psychology*, 12 (1): 75–85.

Thorne, B. (1988) 'Psychotherapy and original sin', *Self and Society*, 16 (5): 207–14.

Thorne, B. (1991) *Person-Centred Counselling: Therapeutic and Spiritual Dimensions*. London: Whurr.

Thorne, B. (1994) 'Developing a spiritual discipline', in D. Mearns (ed.), *Developing Person-Centred Counselling*. London: Sage. pp. 44–7.

Thorne, B. (1998) *Person-Centred Counselling and Christian Spirituality: the Secular and the Holy*. London: Whurr.

Tick, E. (1992) 'Attending the soul', *Voices*, 28 (2): 7–8.

Tillich, P. (1952) *The Courage To Be*. Newhaven and London: Yale University Press.

Tornatore, N.V. and Tornatore, R. (1977) 'The paranormal event in psychotherapy: a survey of 609 psychiatrists', *Psychic*, 7: 34–7.

Totton, N. and Edmondson, E. (1988) *Reichian Growth Work*. Dorset: Prism.

Valla, J-P. and Prince, R.H. (1989) 'Religious experiences as self-healing mechanisms', in C.A. Ward (ed.), *Altered States of Consciousness and Mental Health, a Cross-Cultural Perspective*. Newbury Park, CA: Sage.

Van Belle, H.A. (1990) 'Rogers' later move towards mysticism, implications for client-centred therapy', in G. Lietaer and R. Van Balen (eds), *Client-Centred and Experiential Psychotherapy in the Nineties*. The Netherlands: University of Leuven.

Vaughan, F. (1986) *The Inward Arc: Healing and Wholeness in Psychotherapy and Spirituality*. California: Shambhala.

Vaughan, F. (1989) 'True and false mystical experiences', *Revision*, 12: 4–10.

Vaughan, F. (1991) 'Spiritual issues in psychotherapy', *Journal of Transpersonal Psychology*, 23 (2): 105–19.

Veness, D. (1990) 'Spirituality in counselling: a view from the other side', *British Journal of Guidance & Counselling*, 18 (3): 250–60.

Vigne, J. (1991) 'Guru and psychotherapist: comparisons from the Hindu tradition', *Journal of Transpersonal Psychology*, 23 (2): 121–37.

Vitz, P. (1993) *Sigmund Freud's Christian Unconscious*. Grand Rapids, MI: Eerdmans.

Walker, A. (1998) *Restoring the Kingdom, the Radical Christianity of the House Church Movement*. Guildford: Eagle.

Wallis, J.H. (1993) *Findings: an Inquiry into Quaker Religious Experience*. London: Quaker Home Service.

Walsh, R. (1989) 'What is a shamen?', *Journal of Transpersonal Psychology*, 21 (1): 1–11.

Walsh, R. (1994) 'The making of a shaman: calling, training and culmination', *Journal of Humanistic Psychology*, 34 (3): 7–30.

Walsh, R. and Vaughan, F. (1994) 'The worldview of Ken Wilber', *Journal of Humanistic Psychology*, 34 (2): 6–21.

Washburn, M. (1990) 'Two patterns of transcendence', *Journal of Humanistic Psychology*, 30 (3): 84–112.

Watson, K.W. (1994) 'Spiritual emergency: concepts and implications for psychotherapy', *Journal of Humanistic Psychology*, 34 (2): 22–45.

Watts, A. (1961) *Psychotherapy East and West*. New York: Pantheon.

West, M. (1983) *The World is Made of Glass*. Sevenoaks: Hodder and Stoughton.

West, W.S. (1985) *Loving Contact*. Leeds: Energy Stream.

West, W.S. (1994) 'Post Reichian therapy', in D. Jones (ed.), *Innovative Therapy: a Handbook*. Buckingham: Open University Press.

West, W.S. (1995a) 'Integrating psychotherapy and healing: an inquiry into the experiences of counsellors and psychotherapists whose work includes healing'. PhD thesis, University of Keele.

West, W.S. (1995b) 'Supervision difficulties for psychotherapists and counsellors whose work includes healing'. Paper presented at First Annual Research Conference of the British Association for Counselling, Birmingham University, 25 February.

West, W.S. (1995c) 'The relevance of Quakerism for counsellors', *The Friends Quarterly*, 28 (5): 222–6.

West, W.S. (1996) 'Using human inquiry groups in counselling research', *British Journal of Guidance and Counselling*, 24 (3): 347–55.

West, W.S. (1997) 'Integrating psychotherapy and healing', *British Journal of Guidance and Counselling*, 25 (3): 291–312.

West, W.S. (1998a) 'Developing practice in a context of religious faith: a study of psychotherapists who are Quakers', *British Journal of Guidance & Counselling*, 26 (3): 365–75.

West, W.S. (1998b) 'Therapy as a spiritual process', in C. Feltham (ed.), *Witness and Vision of Therapists*. London: Sage. pp. 158–79.

West, W.S. (1998c) 'Critical subjectivity: use of self in counselling research', *Counselling*, 9 (3): 228–30.

West, W.S. (1998d) 'Spirituality and work', *The Friends Quarterly*, 31 (3): 138–42.

West, W.S. (1999a) 'Counselling as a spiritual space'. In *Counselling and Creation*, Proceedings of the 6th Annual International Counselling Conference, School of Education, Durham University.

West, W.S. (1999b) 'Eclecticism and integration in humanistic therapy', in S. Palmer and R. Woolfe (eds), *Eclectic and Integrative Counselling and Psychotherapy*. London: Sage.

West, W.S. (1999c) 'Supervision difficulties and dilemmas for counsellors and psychotherapists around healing and spirituality', in B. Lawton and C. Feltham (eds), *Taking Supervision Forward: Dilemmas, Insights and Trends*. London: Sage.

Whitmore, D. (1996) 'The psychospiritual and the transpersonal', *Self & Society*, 24 (4): 26–9.

Wilber, K. (1975) 'Psychologia perennis: the spectrum of consciousness', *Journal of Transpersonal Psychology*, 7 (2): 105–32.

Wilber, K. (1979a) 'Eye to eye: the relationship between science, reason and religion and its effect on transpersonal psychology', *Revision*, Winter/Spring: 3–26.

Wilber, K. (1979b) 'A developmental view of consciousness', *Journal of Transpersonal Psychology*, 11 (1): 1–21.

Wilber, K. (1980) *The Atman Project*. Illinois: Quest.

Wilber, K. (1983) *A Sociable God: Towards a New Understanding of Religion*. Boulder, CO: Shambhala.

Wilber, K. (1990) 'Two patterns of transcendence: a reply to Washburn', *Journal of Humanistic Psychology*, 30 (3): 113–36.

Willis, R. (1992a) 'Initiation into healing', *Doctor–Healer Network Newsletter*, 3: 9–11.

Willis, R. (1992b) 'What makes a healer?', *International Journal of Alternative and Complementary Medicine*, November: 11.

Wilson, B.R. (ed.) (1981) *The Social Impact of New Religious Movements*. New York: Rose of Sharon.

Winkleman, M. (1989) 'A cross-cultural study of shamanic healers', *Journal of Psychoactive Drugs*, 21 (1): 17–24.

Yalom, I.D. (1980) *Existential Psychotherapy*. New York: Basic Books.

Young, C. (1988) 'New Age Spirituality', *Self & Society*, 16 (5): 195–201.

Young Friends General Meeting (1998) 'Who do we think we are? Young Friends commitment and belonging'. Swarthmore Lecture, Quaker Home Service, London.

Index